ST. FRANCIS and POPE FRANCIS
Prayer, Poverty, and Joy in Jesus

ST. FRANCIS
and

POPE FRANCIS

PRAYER, POVERTY, AND JOY IN JESUS

ALAN SCHRECK, Ph.D.

Our Sunday Visitor Publishing Division
Our Sunday Visitor, Inc.
Huntington, Indiana 46750

Dedication

*To all faithful followers of St. Francis,
especially my friends and colleagues, past
and present, at Franciscan University:
the friars of the Third Order Regular of
St. Francis of Penance, the Franciscan
Sisters T.O.R. of Penance of the Sorrowful
Mother, and Fr. Conrad Harkins, O.F.M.*

TABLE OF CONTENTS

INTRODUCTION

Jorge Mario Bergoglio made an immediate impression when he chose the name of a medieval saint, Francis of Assisi, upon his election as pope of the Catholic Church. How apropos that the first Jesuit pope and the first pope from the Western Hemisphere should also choose an unprecedented papal name! This book will compare the life and teaching of Pope Francis and those of his namesake, especially exploring what we can learn from them about conversion and discipleship, that is, about following Jesus. Is it possible to find a common message from two persons living eight centuries apart?

The world today is so much different from that of St. Francis. How do we compare a man who wrote relatively little — who is known more through the remembrances and tales of his followers — with one whose every public word is published online almost immediately and who regularly sends "tweets"? How do we compare a person who, following the Holy Spirit's leadings, ended up founding a new religious "way" with a person formed in a rich religious tradition, the Society of Jesus?

Francis of Assisi, in the final years of his short life, passed on to others the leadership of his young order. Jorge Bergoglio, after years of faithful but relatively obscure service to his order and to the Church, was raised to archbishop of one of the world's largest cities and then, when he was preparing to retire from that post, was elected chief shepherd of the Catholic Church. There are many differences, and the most obvious is that St. Francis's life and ministry were completed long ago, while Pope Francis's papal ministry, at this writing, is still in its early stages — a "work in progress."

Despite these differences, there are many evident similarities between St. Francis and Pope Francis. Perhaps the most significant is how quickly both men captured the attention and sparked the imaginations of the people of their times. The religious communities of consecrated (celibate) men and women and groups of lay people who sought to imitate and follow St. Francis blossomed and flourished even in his lifetime. Pope Francis was named "Person of the Year" by *Time* magazine just months after his election. The world is fascinated with both these men.

Hans Urs von Balthasar reflected on the "secret" and the source of St. Francis's appeal, which has not diminished in the eight hundred years since he lived:

> Everything depends on the awareness we have of our Christianity. For Francis, to be a Christian was something just as immense, certain and as star-tlingly glorious as to be a human being, a youth, a man. And because being a Christian is eternal be-ing and eternal youth, without danger of wither-ing or resignation, his immediate joy was deeper. Not one single year separated him from Christ, the one who had become flesh; from the manger; from the Cross. For him, not one speck of dust had settled on the freshness of the wonder in the passage of time. [1]

Here is the critical and closest point of contact between St. Francis and Pope Francis: their sense of the immediacy of the Gospel that flows from their awareness of the closeness of God to us through the coming and the presence of Jesus Christ. It is also the source of the joy that is evident in the lives and messages of both. Pope Francis spoke of this joy in an interview in December 2013, in which he was asked to reflect on "What does Christmas mean for you?"

> It is the encounter with Jesus. God has always sought out his people, led them, looked after them and promised always to be close to them....
>
> This is why Christmas gives us so much joy. We don't feel alone any more. God has come down to be with us. Jesus became one of us and suffered

the worst death for us, that of a criminal on the Cross....

The message announced to us in the Gospels is a message of joy. The evangelists described a joyful event to us. They do not discuss about the unjust world and how God could be born into such a world.... The (first) Christmas was not a condemnation of social injustice and poverty; it was an announcement of joy. Everything else [is] conclusions we draw. Some are correct, others are less so, and others still are ideologized. Christmas is joy, religious joy, God's joy, an inner joy of light and peace....[2]

One indication of the central importance of joy for Pope Francis, and not just for the Christmas season, is that he chose it as a central theme of his first apostolic exhortation, on evangelization, *Evangelii Gaudium* ("The Joy of the Gospel").

One might argue, though, that the theme that St. Francis chose to emphasize was following Jesus in poverty and humility. Again Pope Francis is right there with St. Francis; in fact, Cardinal Bergoglio indicated that identification with the poor and the "poor Christ" was the foremost reason for his choosing the name Francis. And his election was certainly an acknowledgment of his genuine humility and the witness of Gospel poverty in his lifestyle as archbishop. These are themes that this book will explore in some depth.

The book's last chapter, "The Profound Un-Theologian," highlights the importance for both the saint and the pope of *living* the Gospel of Jesus. Though Pope Francis, as a Jesuit, is theologically astute and well trained, he has made it a point to see that his papal teaching, especially in his homilies and audiences, is accessible to everyone, as St. Francis did whenever he preached. Controversies have arisen over some of Pope Francis's responses to questions that have led people to speculate on whether or not he intends to revise some traditional Catholic teaching or pastoral practices. One of the pope's responsibilities is to review areas of the Catholic Church's life and structure. He has chosen eight cardinals to serve as close advisers. He has called for a synod of bishops to discuss marriage and the family. From the perspective of faith, there is no reason for concern over the course Pope Francis has taken or will take.

Like St. Francis, Pope Francis is first and foremost a loyal son of the Catholic Church. Like St. Francis, his mission is not to change the Church in anything essential in her nature or structure but to renew the Church. Like St. Francis, to do this he relies on the guidance of the Holy Spirit. Unlike St. Francis, though, as the vicar of Christ, Pope Francis is blessed with God's guidance and wisdom in a particular way by virtue of his office. As noted, Pope Francis is seeking God's wisdom through consultation with others, as well as through his own prayer and insight. Meanwhile, he has handled some thorny questions deftly and even humorously, such as when he was asked if the Church would have women cardinals in the future. He responded: "I don't know where this idea sprang from. Women in the Church must be valued, not 'clericalised.' Whoever thinks of women as cardinals suffers a bit from clericalism."[3]

St. Francis and Pope Francis each represent in his own time a "fresh breeze" blowing in the Church, an expression of the newness of the Holy Spirit's action in each age of the Church. And yet this breeze in our day is also a reminder of the timeless witness and message of the saints of old, as Pope Francis has called to mind in taking St. Francis of Assisi as a special patron for his pontificate.

CHAPTER 1
FOLLOWING JESUS

Francis of Assisi is assuredly one of the best-known and most widely admired figures in the history of Christianity. There have probably been more biographies written about St. Francis than any other Catholic saint. This book is not a biography but a reflection on what St. Francis, and his namesake, Pope Francis, have to tell us about following Jesus.

The fundamental reason why the Catholic Church declares anyone a saint (the process known as canonization) is that the person has fulfilled the "great" or "new" commandment of Jesus — to love God above all and to love one's neighbors as God loves them (see Matthew 22:36–39; John 13:34). All the accounts of Francis of Assisi's life testify to his extraordinary sanctity. G.K. Chesterton, in his biography of St. Francis, famously remarked:

> He honored all men, that is, he not only loved but respected them all. What gave him his extraordinary personal power was this: that from the Pope to the beggar, from the Sultan of Syria in his pavilion to the ragged robbers crawling out of the wood, there was never a man who looked into those brown burning eyes without being certain that Francis Bernardone was really interested in him, in his own individual inner life from the cradle to the grave; that he himself was valued and taken seriously. [4]

I have met two people who are on the road to being declared saints: Pope John Paul II and Mother Teresa of Calcutta. In my very brief moments with them, I was struck by exactly what Chesterton says of St. Francis: that they were genuinely interested in me, and that I was valued and totally accepted by them, just as I was. As Pope Francis said in his homily on Divine Mercy Sunday, 2013: "For God we are not numbers, we are important, indeed we are the most important thing to him; even if we are sinners we are what is closest to his heart."

There are many great saints in the history of the Catholic Church, but no pope has ever chosen the name Francis until now. Practically every pope has chosen a traditional name in the sense of "used before" or at least the name of a saint who was prominent in early Christianity. Jorge Mario Bergoglio broke with convention in taking the name Francis. But why Francis? And as so many asked at the time the choice was announced, "Which Francis?" (Of Assisi? Xavier? De Sales?) Pope Francis provided the answer within a few days of his election when he addressed six thousand journalists and other media correspondents.

> Some people wanted to know why the Bishop of Rome wished to be called Francis. Some thought of Francis Xavier, Francis De Sales, and also Francis of Assisi. I will tell you the story.
>
> During the election, I was seated next to the Archbishop Emeritus of São Paolo and Prefect Emeritus of the Congregation for the Clergy, Cardinal Claudio Hummes: a good friend, a good friend! When things were looking dangerous, he encouraged me. And when the votes reached two thirds, there was the usual applause, because the Pope had been elected. And he gave me a hug and a kiss, and said: "Don't forget the poor!" And those words came to me: the poor, the poor.

Then, right away, thinking of the poor, I thought of Francis of Assisi. Then I thought of all the wars, as the votes were still being counted, till the end. Francis is also the man of peace. That is how the name came into my heart: Francis of Assisi.

For me, he is the man of poverty, the man of peace, the man who loves and protects creation; these days we do not have a very good relationship with creation, do we? He is the man who gives us this spirit of peace, the poor man.... How I would like a Church which is poor and for the poor![5]

Immediately after Pope Francis's election, I was asked the same questions by a local media correspondent: why "Pope Francis" and *which* Francis? Of course, my response was mere speculation, but I said that the pope might well be thinking of Francis of Assisi because he is so well-known, he loved the poor and marginalized, and he was a man who stood for peace and harmony in a time of conflict and social unrest. Perhaps many others had the same sense of the pope's choice, even before he himself explained it. Above all, the pope is the vicar — that is, the representative — of Christ, and if a pope has to choose any saint who represented and reflected Jesus Christ, Francis of Assisi is certainly a worthy choice.

WHO IS ST. FRANCIS?

St. Francis is universally known and admired, but who was he? Today we can't avoid the question of what and how much we actually know about Francis of Assisi, considering the nature of the medieval sources. This is the "Franciscan question." Some scholars claim that it is impossible to reconstruct a reliable historical account of Francis's life because all of the sources reflect the perspectives and biases of their authors. Even Francis's own writings were written on particular occasions for different purposes. They were not intended to tell about his life, like an autobiography.

Nonetheless, some recent scholars have produced important biographies of Francis of Assisi. One of them, Dominican scholar Augustine Thompson explains:

> ... [A]s for Jesus in the first century, the sources for Francis in the twelfth to thirteenth centuries are much better than those for any other spiritual leader of his age (e.g., Dominic or Valdes) and, unlike Jesus, we have actual writing by Francis — in fact, a large corpus of them.... [B]ut there is no uninterpreted Francis. That includes the Francis of this book[6]

Another is French scholar André Vauchez, who comments in the preface to his biography of Francis of Assisi:

> ... Francis is neither a myth nor a legendary person, even if many legends were written about him in the middle ages, and there is no reason that he should remain more out of reach than his contemporaries like Saint Louis or Frederick II, both of whom have been the subject of remarkable biographies. [7]

Both Thompson and Vauchez observe that the greatest challenge, besides properly evaluating the sources, is to recognize that Francis lived in a much different world whose way of thinking, culture, and values were far different from our own. To understand St. Francis rightly, we must attempt to understand him in the context of his time and culture, so as to avoid anachronistically interpreting Francis as addressing concerns of our own times, such as ecology and present-day cultural and political issues.

Nonetheless, St. Francis of Assisi's life has touched and affected people over the centuries and continues to do so, as the choice of his name by Pope Francis testifies. André Vauchez acknowledges that the impact that Francis of Assisi has had for generations is not based solely on the "historical" Francis as he existed in his time and culture, but that it also comes from the stories, the tales (*legendae*) about Francis that reflect the impression he left on his followers and the impact he had on their lives. Vauchez calls this Francis's *Nachleben* — "after life" — "the different perceptions of his person and life by his contemporaries and those interested in him through the ages."[8]

It has been said (and not only by Franciscans) that Francis was so totally conformed to Jesus that he became the most perfect image of Christ since Mary and the apostles. This is reflected in the characteristics of Francis of Assisi that are not so closely bound to his time and culture, such as his personality, his character and virtues, and his faith.

For example, my first adult introduction to St. Francis was in my junior year of college, when I was assigned to read *The Little Flowers of St. Francis* (the *Fioretti*) for a Church history class. Scholars pretty much agree that this collection of stories is a blend of tales with a widely varying degree of historical credibility.[9] However, for generations Catholics have treasured the *Fioretti* because it refreshingly conveys the spirit of St. Francis — his originality and radical following of Christ. In reading the stories I was captivated by St. Francis's brotherliness and his zeal for the Lord, and I was amused by the uniqueness and eccentricities of his followers, like Brother Juniper. I was hooked on St. Francis.

My point is that while it is important to try to determine what the historical Francis was really like, we cannot easily distinguish this Francis from the many portrayals and tales of St. Francis whose historical accuracy is difficult or impossible to determine. For example, one of the most disputed issues, at least among Franciscans, concerns what St. Francis taught about poverty and how it is to be lived. (This book focuses on Francis's own poor life but not on those disputes.)

However, in most instances there is substantial agreement among all the accounts about what St. Francis stood for, even though scholars may disagree about some historical facts. For example, Francis of Assisi gloried in the created world, seeing it as God's handiwork and as a gift to humankind. Also it is evident that Francis had a unique love for all of God's creatures. Scholars debate whether Francis actually preached a sermon to the birds or tamed the fierce wolf of Gubbio.[10] They note that it was common for miraculous occurrences to be attributed to saints as a way of expressing devotion or of promoting devotion to the saints. However, we know St. Francis's view of the glory of creation because no one questions that he authored the "Canticle of the Creatures," glorifying God in his "brothers and sisters" — the sun, the moon, the stars, wind, water, fire, the earth, and even bodily death.

Likewise, some scholars dispute whether St. Francis received the sacred stigmata — the visible wounds of Jesus — on his body toward the end of his life, but few if any would question whether Francis of Assisi's life was totally conformed to Jesus crucified, which brought him such intense sorrow and such great joy at our salvation.

When Christians speak of the "historical Jesus," it is essential to believe that he performed mighty works (miracles), cast out demons, and conquered death by his bodily resurrection. All these reveal his identity as the Christ, the Savior of the world and the divine, only-begotten Son of God who "became flesh and dwelt among us" (John 1:14). St. Francis was a disciple of Jesus, and he would be recognized as a great disciple and a great saint even if in his life on earth he worked no cures and performed no miraculous deeds. In fact, to some extent St. Francis's accomplishments in this regard are modest. He embraced and gave alms to a leper as well as ministering to many lepers, but he did not heal any of them. He went on a missionary journey to witness the Gospel of Jesus Christ to the sultan, but he did not convert him. Does this matter? Any miracles attributed to St. Francis of Assisi are somehow secondary. What is important is the way he lived as a disciple of Jesus Christ.

The only things historical that would affect the credibility and impact of St. Francis are, for example, if it were demonstrated that he really didn't courageously live complete poverty with a joyful spirit (that he actually was a somber, irritable person), or if his love of creation was shown to be a sham, or if it were known that he didn't constantly turn to God in prayer and respond promptly to the inspiration of the Holy Spirit. No, all of the accounts of St. Francis's life unanimously attest to his zealous love of God and to his virtues and exemplary character. In short, all that really matters is that St. Francis was radically holy — a true and faithful disciple of Jesus Christ.

Of course, if Francis of Assisi had not possessed extraordinary and attractive virtues and character qualities, he would not have made such an impact on his time and ours. Personality, those human traits that make a person unique, does affect a person's social influence, and this was certainly true of Francis of Assisi. The greatest pitfalls in describing the virtue, character traits, and personality of Francis are, as I see it, reductionism and omission. It is very easy to reduce Francis by overly stressing or identifying him with a particular trait or quality. This is all too common: images abound portraying Francis as *just* a nature-lover, or a starry-eyed flower-child of the thirteenth century, or a reformer, quietly rebelling against a worldly, institutional Church.

Likewise, it is just as easy to portray Francis in a broader, more balanced way but to omit some elements that are essential to his identity and mission, such as his commitment to the Catholic Church and her sacraments and devotions.

Another danger, mentioned earlier, is a failure to understand Francis in the context of his time and culture — as a Catholic from a bourgeois merchant family living in a small city in Umbria, Italy, in the late twelfth and early thirteenth centuries. This is where reading various modern biographies and historical studies can be helpful.

I have mentioned that this book is not a biography. For this I recommend that of Omer Englebert (for a popular, non-scholarly presentation), and those of Raoul Manselli, Augustine Thompson, O.P., and André Vauchez (all more scholarly and academic in approach but well-written). Even better would be to read some of Francis's own writings and the early biographies and reflections on his life, which may be found in the multi-volume series from New City Press *St. Francis of Assisi: Early Documents* (begin with volume 1, *The Saint*) and in Marion A. Habig's classic, *St. Francis of Assisi Omnibus of Sources.*

At the risk of omission, I would like to mention some aspects of the life and faith of St. Francis that stand out to me and are also, in some cases, apparent in the life of Pope Francis. A number of these themes will be developed further in this book as particularly important in understanding what St. Francis (and Pope Francis) tell us about encountering and following Jesus.

GETTING TO KNOW FRANCIS OF ASSISI

What was St. Francis like — his personality and his character? We know little about his early life. There is no indication that he was particularly pious as a child or adolescent. The only stories of his youth that give us clues to Francis's character are from his teenage years, when it appears that he was well-liked because he freely spent money for his friends to feast and party. (Francis worked for his father, a well-to-do cloth merchant.) Francis was naturally generous, though it is not clear whether it was with his father's money or his own. Probably both.

The young Francis also possessed a natural compassion for and sensitivity to others. A characteristic story describes the time a poor man came into the family shop to beg alms but left because Francis was busy with a customer. Francis, apparently feeling guilty for ignoring the man, bolted from the shop, found him, and gave him a generous sum. Three early accounts record, "Because of this incident, he [Francis] resolved in his heart, from then on, never to refuse a request from anyone asking in the name of so great a Lord."[11] Even in his youth Francis understood the value, dignity, and importance of each person, and in particular the poor and those in need. On another occasion Francis gave away his splendid military attire and armor to a poorer knight.[12]

As these incidents indicate, Francis had a tendency to be spontaneous and even at times impetuous. Chesterton thinks Francis was practical, in the sense of having "a preference for prompt effort and energy over doubt and delay." Some have portrayed Francis as somewhat of a dreamer, "yet he was the very reverse of a dreamer.... [H]e was very emphatically a man of action."[13]

Francis's propensity for actions over words is reflected in a popular phrase attributed to him that was articulated by Pope Francis in a speech given at St. Paul Outside-the-Walls on April 14, 2013:

> One cannot proclaim the Gospel of Jesus without the tangible witness of one's life. Those who listen to us and observe us must be able to see in our actions what they hear from our lips, and so give glory to God! I am thinking now of some advice that St. Francis of Assisi gave his brothers: "Preach the Gospel and, if necessary, use words."[14]

It is ironic that this phrase, "Preach the Gospel and, if necessary, use words," which is widely quoted and even emblazoned on tee-shirts at Franciscan University, is not a saying of St. Francis found in any existing manuscript. Nevertheless, it does accurately portray the life and message of St. Francis: that he valued action — *living* the Gospel — over words (see chapter 7, on mission). Pope Francis too emphasizes that living the Gospel, not merely talking about it, is decisive.

One of the most distinctive and original characteristics of Francis of Assisi was the courtesy that he extended to all people.[15] Some have referred to this as Francis's courtliness or his nobility — even dressed in rags, there was something about him that was noble. Perhaps this stemmed from the fact that Francis belonged to a wealthy merchant class that was aspiring to the prestige of the nobility. This would also explain why the young Francis dressed so ostentatiously and threw lavish banquets for his friends. Or perhaps this reflected the influence of chivalry and the romantic culture of southern France — Francis could speak and sing in French dialect, and it seems likely that he was named in honor of that country.

Like other youth of his day, Francis was influenced by the stories of heroism — the *chansons de geste*, songs of great deeds — and of courtly romance that were sung by the troubadours. He wanted to be a knight, aspiring to worldly fame and glory. Even when he was captured and imprisoned in his first battle, with neighboring Perugia, he retained his good humor. One of the earliest accounts of Francis states that a prisoner "rebuked him as insane for being cheerful in prison. Francis replied vigorously: 'What do you think will become of me? Rest assured I will be worshipped through the whole world.'"[16]

We can understand why Francis was portrayed as a dreamer with an inflated ego, but this does not do him jus-

life. For example, immediately after this statement Francis befriended a fellow prisoner who was being ostracized by the others, and he urged those others to accept him. So Francis's prison stay reveals one of his strengths: his mood was not controlled by his external circumstances. He was typically buoyant and positive, even in adversity.

Before his conversion Francis sometimes appeared narcissistic and vain (for example, in the way he dressed), but after he encountered Christ, he retained his noble, chivalrous spirit and directed it to a different end. As a knight serving Christ Jesus, his lady was now Lady Poverty. He still aspired to be a troubadour, full of song and good cheer, or a *jongleur* — a jester or juggler — but now he became a troubadour or herald of the Great King and a fool for Christ. In this we detect the childlike simplicity of Francis and the enthusiasm that even difficult circumstances, opposition, and suffering could not dampen or at least not totally quench. Along with all of these, we note his instinctive appreciation of beauty, especially the beauty of God's creation. (And those who have visited Assisi and the region of Umbria know that natural beauty abounds!)

Perhaps the quality that best summarizes the plethora of natural virtues that Francis of Assisi possessed is *magnanimity*. Pope Francis has spoken about this quality, which well describes Francis of Assisi:

> What does being magnanimous mean? It means having a great heart, having greatness of mind; it means having great ideals, the wish to do great things, to respond to what God asks us. Hence also, for this very reason, to do well the routine things of every day and all the daily actions, tasks, meetings with people; doing the little everyday things with a great heart open to God and to others....[17]

Francis had great ideals and a great heart — there was nothing "small" about his goals, his giving, or his values. And yet he realized that these could only be accomplished by doing little things well — the ordinary things of everyday life. Pope Francis calls magnanimity the "virtue of the great and the small" and explains the source of this magnanimity in words that apply particularly well to St. Francis:

> And it is important to find this magnanimity with Jesus, in contemplating Jesus. Jesus is the one who opens windows for us on the horizon. Magnanimity means walking with Jesus, with a heart attentive to what Jesus tells us....[18]

A final virtue that enabled St. Francis to persevere in accomplishing what he did (and without which he could not have done it) is *courage*. Francis is often pictured, as is Jesus, as gentle, "meek and mild," but it should not be construed that either of them lacked courage. Jesus insisted that those who follow him would need to pick up their crosses daily (Luke 9:23), willing to accept, as he did, sacrifice, opposition, rejection, and even death. This requires courage. Did this well-to-do, idealistic young man, Francis, have this kind of courage? This can only be answered for Francis, as for us, a step at a time.

At each stage of his life, Francis exhibited a courage that Pope Francis often speaks of — *parrhesia*, in Greek — that is, a "holy boldness" to do and say what needs to be said and done, flowing from a childlike confidence and trust in God. St. Paul taught that God chooses the weak to shame the strong, and the foolish to shame the wise (1 Corinthians 1:27). Francis acknowledged that he was a "*minor*" — a little one — whose strength came solely from God. This is honest, true humility, and it never prevented St. Francis from pursuing and doing God's will once he understood it.

To be humble, knowing your own weaknesses and limitations, and yet to step out to accomplish what you think must be done (what God calls you to do), is *parrhesia*. Francis of Assisi had this humble courage, which produced in him a remarkable boldness and freedom to live and act as he was convinced God was calling him to do — even when his family and much of Assisi thought that this rich young merchant had gone mad in abandoning his worldly life and becoming, seemingly, a vagrant, a beggar. "Always being free to choose goodness is demanding," Pope Francis has said, but it makes us "into people with a backbone who can face life, people with courage and patience (*parrhesia* and *ypomoné*)."[19]

But how did Francis turn from being a rich young businessman, the popular *King of Youth*, to be a wholehearted, poor disciple of Jesus? In the next chapter we will reflect on the process of Francis of Assisi's conversion.

CHAPTER 2

CONVERSION: THE TASK OF A LIFETIME

To be a Christian requires conversion. One does not become a disciple of Jesus Christ without a decision to follow him and the change that this involves. But conversion, while it can initially be a dramatic renunciation of sin and turning toward God, is also an ongoing choice that unfolds over time through prayer, repentance, forgiveness, and seeking God's will. And so even those baptized as infants who grow up practicing their faith must make a decision to live for Christ, and they must keep making that choice as they grow in faith. As the *Catechism* says, "Christ's call to conversion continues to resound in the lives of Christians. This *second conversion* is an uninterrupted task for the whole Church" (CCC 1428). The phrase "intentional disciple," popular lately in Christian circles, highlights the truth that following Jesus, being a disciple, requires conscious choices and decisions that are purposeful and that result in action.

When Catholics are asked about their conversion, they will often respond, "I'm not a convert; I've always been Catholic." On the other hand, many will tell about some important moment when they encountered God or, more specifically, Jesus, and the difference that has made in their lives. These moments, which in big and small ways can occur over a lifetime, support and drive an individual's ongoing surrender to Christ in a life fully conformed to him. It is primarily in this latter sense that we will speak of conversion in this chapter.

Pope Francis mentions a particular event that changed the direction of his life when he was seventeen. On September 21, 1953, the Feast of St. Matthew — also the first day of spring in Argentina and a day of celebration for students — he suddenly felt that he should go to confession. A practicing Catholic, he stopped at his parish church on the way to a festival, and a priest he did not know unexpectedly appeared and heard his confession.

Pope Francis describes two things about this experience that had a great impact on him. The first is his sense that the priest was there waiting for him, which enabled the pope to perceive that God is always "there first," waiting to forgive us and to be with us. When Pope Francis reflects on the parable of the merciful Father (also known as the parable of the prodigal son), as he did on Divine Mercy Sunday 2013, there is an amazing depth of insight and power as he describes how the father in the parable did not just "happen" to be looking out and catch sight of his youngest son at a distance. No, the pope says that the father had gone out every day, anticipating his son's return and waiting to catch sight of him.

So God the Father watches for each person, with great love, to come to him for forgiveness and healing. It is not that we must search for God, who is hiding himself; God is always waiting there for us when we turn to him, as young Jorge Bergoglio did when he went to confession that day in 1953.

The other result of the experience was that, after that confession, "I felt something had changed. I was not the same," the pope said. "I had heard something like a voice, or a call. I was convinced that I should become a priest."[20] On another occasion Pope Francis said of this incident "that it was not only the 'astonishment of the encounter' which revealed to him his religious vocation, but the compassionate way in

which God called him   in such a way that, over time, it became a source of inspiration for his own ministry."[21]

Christian conversion is, for Pope Francis, first and foremost the result of an encounter with a person — the person
of the Lord Jesus Christ. After telling of his own encounter
with Jesus, Pope Francis reflected:

> The Lord is waiting for us. Moreover, when we seek
> him, we discover that he is waiting to welcome us,
> to offer us his love. And this fills your heart with
> such wonder that you can hardly believe it, and
> this is how your faith grows — through encounter
> with a Person, through encounter with the Lord.
>
> Some people will say, "No, I prefer to read
> about faith in books!" It is important to read about
> faith, but look, on its own this is not enough! What
> is important is our encounter with Jesus, our en-
> counter with him, and this is what gives you faith
> because he is the one who gives it to you![22]

Pope Francis had an encounter with Jesus, through the
sacrament of reconciliation, that clearly indicated to him his
vocation to be a priest. With young Francis of Assisi, it appears that his conversion to Christ occurred, and his vocation
was revealed, over an extended period of time. It unfolded in
many steps. This is also the experience of many Christians.

ST. FRANCIS'S CONVERSION

The common impression of St. Francis of Assisi's conversion,
which resulted in his becoming a radical disciple of Christ
and a religious leader, is that it all happened in one day when
he was praying in a dilapidated country church dedicated to
St. Damian. There Jesus spoke to Francis from the crucifix
and told him to "rebuild my church," which Francis proceeded to do. This experience with the Lord was a critical mo-

ment in Francis's conversion, but his movement toward God certainly didn't begin or end there.

Unlike the conversion of St. Paul, for example, Francis of Assisi's spiritual journey was considerably more gradual and winding, and in many respects his conversion continued throughout his life. (I am very familiar with this because the Franciscans who sponsor the university where I teach embrace "ongoing conversion" as their particular charism — at the heart of their preaching and their lives.)

What about Francis's spiritual journey? What Francis himself says about his early life is summed up in the words of his "Testament" (written shortly before his death): "when I was in sin."[23] We don't know exactly what Francis's sins were, though all the early accounts portray him as a fun-loving, worldly spendthrift with a generous and compassionate heart. Like many other young men his age, he wanted to win fame and glory as a knight. It is in this aspiration to worldly greatness that Francis's conversion to a new way of life began.

At age twenty-two, Francis equipped himself to join a local army going to war against neighboring Perugia. The tensions of such conflict were part of life in the Assisi of Francis's youth. It is likely that Francis learned to build and repair stone walls as a teenager by pitching in to fortify the walls of his city in view of recent or impending attacks. Later, as a young man, Francis purchased a horse and armor and set out to battle, but he was captured and imprisoned. Nonetheless, he kept his spirits high as a captive and even predicted that he was destined to do great things. After his release, either as a result of ransom or because he was sick, or both, Francis, worn down, suffered a long illness.[24] During the illness, which lasted from 1203 to the spring of 1205, he was listless and depressed.[25]

Some accounts see this period as the beginning of his conversion. All of the things that normally brought Francis joy, such as the beauty of nature and earthly things, lost their appeal for a time.[26] Thompson believes that Francis may have been suffering from what today is called post-traumatic stress disorder, in the aftermath of his war experience and imprisonment.[27]

During this time, the early biographies report, Francis had unusual dreams. In one dream he was in a house full of weapons, auguring future military success. At this his spirit revived, and he prepared to set out on another military expedition. He got as far as Spoleto, a day's journey away, when that night he had another strange dream (or perhaps a conversation with someone during which he worked out his feelings and misgivings — the sources are unclear). Francis was confronted with the question of whom he was really serving in taking up arms: the master (God?) or a servant (the rulers of this world?). As a result of this, he suddenly decided to return to Assisi. Though the early accounts differ, in one chronology Francis stopped in Foligno on his return, sold his horse and military attire, and walked back to Assisi. His military career was at an end and his future uncertain.

What was this young man Francis experiencing during this period of his life? Did he understand that God was seeking to guide him, or were his dreams and questions, like ours, somewhat opaque and certainly not absolutely clear in their meaning? I agree with Augustine Thompson's view that, in this period of Francis's life, he was struggling to understand himself and his future direction. His war experience and subsequent illness had shaken his confidence that he was destined for greatness in the world, though these trials and uncertainties could not annihilate his innate good humor and idealism. He aspired to serve "the master" — to seek the highest good — whatever that meant.

His unexpected return to Assisi, without horse or armor, certainly raised many eyebrows. Even though Francis tried to continue his life where he had left off, all of the accounts agree that he was not the same. After throwing a party for his friends, instead of going out to carouse with them he hung back alone. They joked that he was mooning over a young lady. In some accounts Francis responded to this in the affirmative, thinking of Lady Poverty, but at this point it is unlikely that Francis had any inkling of his vocation.

He had also lost interest in his profession, and he began to give more liberally to beggars and those in need. There was increased tension with his father, who was still upset that his son had either lost or squandered the money from selling his horse and arms at Foligno. (Thompson believes that he had offered the money to the priest at the dilapidated chapel of San Damiano and had flung it on a window ledge when the priest refused to take it.[28])

How did Francis deal with these feelings and find a direction for his life? He wanted to break with his profligate past, but how was this to be done? Whatever the state of his soul, he chose the remedy of the age (and of the Church) for expiating personal sin. He performed the traditional works of penance: almsgiving, prayer, and bodily mortification.[29]

This decision to repent and do penance for his past sins could be seen as the first step in Francis's conversion to becoming a serious, intentional follower of Jesus Christ. Pope Francis has observed that when God has the true and proper place in a person's life, that person will worship God and God alone. (This is the first of God's commandments: "I am the LORD your God.... You shall have no other gods before me" [Exodus 20:2–3; Deuteronomy 5: 6–7].) "Worshiping the Lord," Pope Francis has said,

> means that we are convinced before him that he is the only God, the God of our lives.... This has a consequence in our lives: we have to empty ourselves of the many small or great idols that we have and in which we take refuge, on which we often seek to base our security....

I would like a question to resound in the
heart of each one of you, and I would like you to
answer it honestly: Have I considered which idol
lies hidden in my life that prevents me from worshipping the Lord? Worshipping is stripping ourselves of our idols, even the most hidden ones, and
choosing the Lord as the center, as the highway of
our lives.[30]

Francis recognized that wealth, pleasure, and fame (or
the desire for fame) had become his idols, obstacles to finding God or at least to finding true meaning in life. His response was to distance himself from his friends, to deny himself those pleasures that had bound him to ease and comfort,
to cease seeking fame through military exploits, and to be
even more generous in giving alms.

The sacrament of reconciliation, commonly called *confession*, is an important avenue of repentance for Catholics.
Though this is not mentioned explicitly in the early biographies of Francis, it is reasonable to assume that this sacrament was part of his repentance. As Pope Francis has said,
so many centuries later, "We must really recognize our sins,
and not present ourselves with a false image.... [W]e have a
treasure: the Saviour Jesus Christ, the Cross of Jesus Christ is
the treasure in which we rejoice, [but let us not forget] to also
confess our sins."[31] And we have seen that it was immediately
after going to confession that the seventeen-year-old Jorge
Bergoglio felt himself to be changed and sensed a strong calling from God to be a priest.

St. Francis also performed another penance that, because of the hardship involved, was a popular form of penance in medieval culture: he went on a pilgrimage. Francis's
pilgrimage, to Rome, brought him to the tomb of St. Peter,
where he threw a lavish offering of coins through the gate,
exchanged his rich clothing with a beggar, and then begged
alms from passersby in broken French.[32] It seems evident that

Francis was groping for a way to change his lifestyle and do penance for his sins. Giving generously of his money to the Church and to those in need and taking on himself the life of the poor seemed to Francis to be a good way to begin.

Francis's troubled search continued when he returned to Assisi. He spent his time wandering about and seeking solitude in caves and small churches, in various stages of disrepair, that dotted the countryside. One of the churches he frequented was San Damiano, just a short hike outside of Assisi. It is thought that one of Francis's earliest prayers came from this period. It is characteristically simple, direct, and reverent:

> Most high, glorious God, enlighten the shadows of my heart and grant unto me a right faith, a certain hope and perfect charity, sense and understanding, Lord, that I may accomplish your holy and true command.[33]

About six months after his return to Assisi, Francis moved out of his home to live at the church of San Damiano, where he became a freelance penitent, or *conversus*, attached to that church.[34] The penitent was an accepted form of medieval Catholic life, and perhaps Francis was advised to do this by his bishop, Guido, or by the priest of San Damiano, Don Peter. Whatever the reason, Francis lodged in or near San Damiano, seeking God's guidance. This guidance came to him in prayer before the Byzantine-style crucifix of San Damiano. Francis heard Christ call him to "repair [or rebuild] my Church." Whether or not Francis saw the lips of the crucified Christ move or heard an interior "voice," the important thing is that God responded to Francis's prayer for direction.

Though he could not grasp the full impact of the word God spoke to him, Francis's response to it was prompt and literal. He collected and begged for stones and began to repair the crumbling chapel, San Damiano. He, and later his companions with him, rebuilt this and at least two other churches, accord ing to the early accounts. Thus the key to this stage of Francis's conversion was obedience, like Noah's response when he heard God call him to build the ark. In the end, the simple, faithful response of Francis to Jesus' call to "rebuild my Church" was to contribute greatly to the restoration of the whole Church and of Western civilization in this era.

Francis's departure from the world took another major step when his father, Pietro di Bernardone, sought restitution for the goods that Francis had sold or given away, particularly his horse and armor. Pietro was angry and very likely embarrassed by his son's inexplicable behavior when Francis withdrew from the family business in order to beg and do penance. Pietro locked Francis up in the family home when he went on a business trip, only to have his wife release Francis before his return.

The tension between Francis and his father was a great trial for Francis as well, though he knew the Lord's warning that those who followed him would create division within their own families (see Matthew 10:34–38). Francis's father wanted to bring his son to court to seek restitution. Since Francis had made himself a ward of the Church as a penitent, Francis and his father appeared before the bishop, instead of a civil court, to adjudicate the matter.

The story of Francis's dramatic gesture of stripping himself, returning all his clothes to his father, and declaring that henceforth he would only say "our Father in heaven" instead of "my father, Pietro di Bernardone" is well-known. (Certainly his flair for the dramatic was one thing that later attracted people to follow Francis.) In his conversion process, Francis felt the need for the public profession of his total allegiance to God and to the Church, as represented by Bishop Guido, who symbolically covered Francis with his own robes and accepted him as a son of the Church. Francis wanted to serve and follow God as his true father, and for him this meant taking the Church as his new family, as represented by the father of his local church, the bishop. Conversion or turning to God meant for Francis turning to the Church as well, for in Catholic theology the Church *is* the body of Christ — the visible presence of Jesus in the world.

It is notable that Francis never left the Catholic Church, as did many other poverty-minded reformers of his time. Rather, Francis's conversion caused him to turn more fully to the Church in trust and love as he submitted his life more completely to God.

Francis's initial conversion, however, was not yet complete. In fact, the key moment of St. Francis's conversion had not yet taken place, even after he renounced the world and placed himself totally in the hands of God and the Church. What more was needed to set Francis securely on his way to a life of following and serving Jesus Christ? There was one great obstacle that God knew needed to be overcome in young Francis's life. Every person has such an obstacle, whether it be a certain fear or a habit of sin that keeps one in bondage, unable to follow Jesus freely.

Francis's obstacles were a fear and a revulsion, closely related. His fear was that in living as a penitent, he might become like a deformed, hunchbacked woman that he either had seen or imagined. His revulsion was for lepers. If he ever saw a person with leprosy or heard the bell of a leper, he would hold his nose and hurry off in another direction. We have little experience of this in our sanitized, affluent Western culture, but I can imagine that my response to coming upon a leper likely would have been the same. In any case, the climax of Francis's initial conversion — perhaps the sign of its accomplishment — was when he found his attitude toward lepers totally changed by God. Francis wrote of this at the very end of his life, in his "Testament":

> This is how the Lord gave me, brother Francis, the power to do penance. When I was in sin the sight

of lepers was too bitter for me. And the Lord him
self led me among them, and I pitied and helped
them. And when I left them I discovered that what
had seemed bitter to me was changed into sweetness in my soul and body. And shortly afterward I
rose and left the world.[35]

Francis here indicates two "stages" in his conversion.
The first is that God led Francis at some point to go among
lepers, and he responded to God's grace and "showed mercy" to them. It is likely that after he had left Bishop Guido
and placed himself under his protection, Francis went to
a leprosarium and by God's grace began to minister to
the lepers in some way. The second work of conversion is
God's change of Francis's heart, making sweet what previously had been bitter. Similarly, when Francis began to beg
for food, at first he was disgusted by "this mess," but then
God enabled him to be thankful and to relish it. Fr. Augustine Thompson, O.P., beautifully describes this climactic
conversion:

> What before was ugly and repulsive now caused
> him delight and joy, not only spiritually, but also
> viscerally and physically. Francis's aesthetic sense,
> so central to his personality, had been trans-
> formed, even inverted. The startled veteran sensed
> himself, by God's grace and no power of his own,
> remade into a different man. Just as suddenly, the
> sins that had been tormenting him seemed to melt
> away, and Francis experienced a kind of spiritual
> rebirth and healing. Not long after this encoun-
> ter, later accounts tell us, perhaps in allegory, that
> Francis was walking down a road and met one of
> these same lepers. He embraced the man in his
> arms and kissed him. Francis's spiritual nightmare
> was over; he had found peace. [36]

Thompson agrees with one of the great modern Franciscan scholars, Raoul Manselli, that the central moment of Francis of Assisi's conversion was this meeting with the leper, which God used to change his heart and his life.[37] Further, Manselli argues that what marked the climax of Francis's initial conversion was his decision to identify himself no longer as a person with a respectable social standing (that is, as a merchant) but as a derelict, an outcast, a nobody. Francis saw the need not just to practice poverty but to change his social status to that of "a man on the fringe of society, a pauper among the poor, a leper among lepers."[38] We will reflect more on this in chapter 4, on poverty. We will also consider more fully later the result, the visible fruit, of Francis's conversion — joy. Manselli observes:

> The change of values ... [in] Francis' life choice, his existential option at the moment of his conversion, continued to work in him. The joy that sprang from his heart and that lived in his song proved that what had been bitter for him came to seem sweet to him. This joy also had a social and even a shock value, for it showed to anyone who was wretched, derelict, or abandoned the precise nature as well as the deep meaning of his or her situation: happiness and unhappiness cannot be reduced ... to an economic common denominator.... Rather, they spring from our interiority, from the depths of our consciousness.[39]

Note that Francis's initial conversion was expressed in a twofold way. The first was a decision to give himself totally to God and to the Church by living a penitential life — identifying himself as a poor penitent, an outcast, and a beggar with no social status. The second, which by the grace of God resulted from the first, was Francis's experience of sweetness, joy, and liberation. Paradoxically, it resulted from a way of life that most people in the world would find depressing, uncomfortable, and burdensome.

Pope Francis speaks frequently about conversion as a personal encounter with Jesus, but he emphasizes that the sign of true conversion is going out with the Gospel of Jesus and living it on the "outskirts" or the fringes of society.[40] Like Francis in his conversion, we are challenged to go out and live our faith, serving those on the edges. Francis's conversion transformed him into a man who no longer retreated into the comfort zone of his affluence but found freedom living and serving as a disciple of Jesus among the poor and the marginalized.

We also see in Francis's conversion story someone who struggled interiorly with feelings of guilt from his past and uncertainty about how to relate to his father and his mother, especially when he had to break from them in order to heed his conscience following God's call. God certainly revealed his will to Francis, but as often happens in our lives, God's call unfolded gradually and not without struggle and uncertainty. Yet there were also moments of clarity and light, which for Francis (as for us) were moments to be treasured, pondered, and built upon. Francis's virtue was that he persevered in seeking God, thus allowing God's work of conversion to unfold and finally to blossom into something beautiful and even magnificent.

What can we learn about conversion from the life of Francis of Assisi and from Pope Francis? First, Christian conversion is all about meeting Jesus Christ, that is, entering into a relationship with God through the God-man, Jesus, and having our lives changed to conform more closely to his life. Pope Francis, in a question-and-answer session with young people, told them:

> … [L]ove Jesus Christ more and more! Our life is a response to his call. May you feel the Lord's presence in your life. He is close to each one of you as a companion, as a friend.…[41]

So the first step of conversion is God's initiative, God's call to enter into a personal relationship with him.

Second, to respond to this invitation to believe in and follow Jesus, a person must consciously renounce and turn away from sin, because sin prevents us from entering into this close relationship with Jesus. The second step, in one word, is to *repent*, as we see St. Francis did when he renounced those things that kept him from wholeheartedly following the Lord.

The third stage of conversion for St. Francis was to undertake a life of penance and mortification, which was a continuing expression of repentance (turning from sin). Francis also prayed for God to forgive his past sins and to guide him in changing the direction of his life.

The fourth stage, related to the last, is to be attentive to God's direction — growing in the capacity to recognize when God is "speaking" and how the Lord is guiding us. This occurs through prayer, discernment, and advice from other spiritually mature people, such as the direction Francis received from his bishop, Guido.

The fifth stage of conversion is to act upon what God has revealed or the direction he has given. This requires the grace of God, as well as human decision and effort. Pope Francis reflected on this road of conversion in his dialogue with young people:

> But it is so beautiful to follow Jesus, to walk in the footsteps of Jesus, that you may then find balance and move forward. And then come even more wonderful moments [that is, like those moments when God "spoke" to Francis in various ways]. But no one must think that there will not be difficult moments in life…. How do you think you can move forward with hardships? It isn't easy; but we must go ahead with strength and with trust in the Lord. With the Lord everything is possible"[42]

CHAPTER 3

PRAYER: A WINDOW INTO THE SOUL

Francis of Assisi experienced an interior restlessness — a search for direction for his life — when he came to recognize the emptiness of his affluent lifestyle and the vanity of his quest for greatness as a soldier. Conscious of his need to seek God's call to him after he abandoned his last military venture and returned to Assisi, he turned to prayer. St. Bonaventure wrote that Francis, having left the hectic pace of the business world, spent his time ardently asking God to reveal to him the direction he should take.[43]

I can imagine St. Francis saying these words of Pope Francis: "I must put myself in the presence of God and, aided by His word, go forward in what He desires." [44]

We can envision Francis of Assisi kneeling before the crucifix at San Damiano, imploring God, as Francis said in an early prayer, to enlighten his darkness and to give him faith, hope, love, understanding, and the ability to do God's will.[45]

Pope Francis, in turn, resonates with St. Francis's longing:

… [P]rayer should somehow be an experience of giving way, or surrendering … where our entire being enters into the presence of God. It is where a dialogue happens, the listening, the transformation. Look to God, but above all feel looked at by God.[46]

Perhaps in kneeling before that crucifix in San Damiano, Francis truly felt that God was looking upon him, hearing his prayer, and at length speaking to him and giving him
the direction he earnestly sought. At any rate, this period of
spiritual searching and prayer led, gradually, to the transformation of his life.

As Francis was touched by God's grace, undergoing a
decisive conversion, prayer became more central to his life.
All of the accounts of Francis by his companions recount how
he loved solitude and constantly gave himself over to prayer.
St. Bonaventure reported that he sought out isolated places
and there prayed at length with such intensity and sorrow —
St. Bonaventure, quoting Romans 8:26, says that it was "with
inexpressible groanings" (NAB) — that the Lord heard him.

On the steep slopes of Mount Subasio, just outside of Assisi, near the Benedictine hermitage known as the Carceri, Francis would retreat with his followers into the little caves and cave-
like enclosures on the slopes to pray. St. Bonaventure records
many instances of St. Francis encountering God in prayer, often
giving Francis a prophetic revelation, such as the assurance of
the forgiveness of his sins, the expansion of his followers to a
"great multitude,"[47] and even a Moses-like reception of the rule
of the order by a direct revelation from God. Bonaventure says
that the Holy Spirit "suggested" the rule to Francis as he prayed
on a mountaintop, accompanied by some brothers.[48]

When Francis was in doubt regarding whether he should
devote himself exclusively to prayer or go about preaching,
he entrusted the discernment of this question to the prayer
of two holy people, Brother Silvester (a priest) and St. Clare.
Both, "through the miraculous revelation of the Holy Spirit,"
came to the same conclusion: "that it was God's good pleasure that Francis should preach as a herald of Christ." [49]

St. Bonaventure devoted the latter chapters in his *Life of
Francis* to different virtues and attributes of Francis that stand
out. In chapter 10, "On His Zeal for Prayer and the Power of

His Prayer," Bonaventure highlighted how Francis was totally open and responsive to the Holy Spirit. "He was accustomed not to pass over negligently any visitation of the Spirit. When it was granted, he followed it, and as long as the Lord allowed, he enjoyed the sweetness offered him." If he was traveling and sensed the presence of the Spirit, he stopped, allowing the visitation to bear fruit, so that as Scripture warns, he did not "accept the grace of God in vain" (2 Corinthians 6:1). Bonaventure also said that Francis frequently experienced ecstasies in prayer that drew him so completely out of himself that he had no idea what was going on around him.[50]

Sometimes Francis would burst into joyful praise to God as Jesus did (Luke 10:21). "The author of the earliest biography of St. Francis of Assisi tells us that, whenever he was full of fervor and needed to give vent to the fire of love in his heart, 'as if drunk in the Spirit,' he would sing in French."[51] At other times, St. Francis would seek out lonely places or abandoned churches to pray, often all night, because he found the Holy Spirit more intimately present there, though he often found himself engaged in horrific struggles with devils, even physically, as they tried to disrupt his prayer. Through his patience and constancy, Francis persevered in prayer and conquered these attacks.[52]

Francis's followers were attracted to him because of his fervor in prayer, and they learned from him. Francis's first disciple, the first whose name we know — Bernard of Quintevalle — was convinced that Francis was truly a godly man worth following because he could see that Francis didn't sleep much and instead prayed throughout the night.

In his chapter on St. Francis's prayer, St. Bonaventure elucidated some of its notable attributes:

- Fervor: "[H]e would fill the groves with sighs, sprinkle the ground with tears, strike his breast with his fist,... groan aloud, imploring the divine mercy for sinners and weeping for the Lord's passion."

- Intimacy: Francis "would converse with the Lord, there he would answer his Judge, he would entreat his Father, there he would entertain his Friend."

- Humility: "When he prayed with the friars, he completely avoided all sputtering, groaning, deep sighs or external movements." He counseled a friar to return from prayer, even if blessed by God in a unique way, "as if he had obtained no new grace."

- Reverence: This was evident when Francis prayed the psalms and other liturgical prayers, and "he wanted to honor with special reverence the Lord's name…. [W]hen he pronounced or heard the name of 'Jesus,' he was filled with joy interiorly and seemed to be altered exteriorly."

- Particular devotions: In the third year before his death, he petitioned the pope to celebrate Christmas at Greccio with a living, true-to-life representation of the birth of Christ in honor of the Lord's incarnation.[53]

It is also revealing to see how St. Francis responded to his disciples' request to teach them to pray, reminiscent of the apostles and Jesus. He reminded them to pray the Our Father. He entreated them to adore Christ in every church throughout the world. He spoke ardently of praising God for his creatures, of honoring priests, and of holding with determination to the Catholic faith. The friars obeyed, Bonaventure tells us, humbly prostrating themselves in prayer and praying as Francis taught them.[54]

THE RICHNESS OF THE PRAYER OF ST. FRANCIS

As a faithful Catholic, Francis had a deep devotion to Jesus in the Eucharist, and he insisted that the friars who could read should pray with the Church, using the Liturgy of the Hours.

He himself would pray the Hours standing erect, even when fatigued or in foul weather when traveling. Liturgical prayer was important, but Francis knew what was later beautifully expressed in Vatican II's *Constitution on the Sacred Liturgy*:

> The spiritual life, however, is not limited solely to participation in the liturgy. The Christian is indeed called to pray with others, but he must also enter into his bedroom to pray to the Father in secret (Matthew 6:6); furthermore, according to the teaching of the apostle, we must pray without ceasing (1 Thessalonians 5:17). We also learn from the same apostle that we must also carry around in our bodies the dying of Jesus, so that the life of Jesus may be made manifest in our mortal flesh (2 Corinthians 4: 10–11).[55]

Who sought to pray at all times, looking for solitude in order to pray to the Father in secret, more fervently than Francis of Assisi? And who, by a penitential life, carried out and made manifest the dying of Jesus more fully than Francis? The liturgical and sacramental prayer in which Francis was immersed with his brothers was rooted in his deep personal relationship with the Father and with Jesus through the Holy Spirit.

This richness of experience of God in prayer is also evident in the life of Pope Francis. Cardinal Bergoglio, soon before his election to the papacy, commented that "sometimes the religious experience in prayer occurs to me when I pray aloud with the rosary or the psalms or when I joyfully celebrate the Eucharist. But the moment when I most savor the religious experience, however long it may be, is when I am before the tabernacle. [56]

Pope Francis admits that he sometimes "allows" himself to fall asleep during that prayer before the tabernacle, but this doesn't concern him, because then he feels "as if I were in someone else's hands, as if God were taking me by the hand." When Pope John Paul II was asked, for his book *Crossing the Threshold of Hope*, how he prayed, he responded that you would have to ask the Holy Spirit, because the pope prays as the Holy Spirit permits him to pray. The same is true of all who pray, because as Pope Francis has often explained, Christian prayer is not just a human act, an act of the will, but the action of God in us. About prayer, Pope John Paul II said that St. Paul got to the heart of the matter when he taught, "We do not know how to pray as we ought, but the Spirit himself intercedes with inexpressible groanings" (Romans 8:26, NAB).[57]

ANOINTED PRAYER

True prayer is "anointed" and led by God. The recorded prayers of St. Francis are clear evidence of this. It perplexes me that more has not been written on the prayers of St. Francis. Nothing teaches us more about who a person really is than how that person prays. It is like a window into the soul, and the prayers of St. Francis, being so numerous, form a picture window!

Jesus taught his followers about prayer in many ways. He told parables about being confident and persevering in approaching our heavenly Father in prayer. Jesus went to the temple and the synagogues and prayed there as a faithful Jew. He spent whole nights alone in prayer. He prayed when healing or blessing food (sometimes multiplying it!), and he offered his great "high priestly" prayer at the Last Supper. At times he burst into spontaneous, exuberant thanks and praise to the Father (see Luke 10:21). And of course, he taught his followers one rote prayer that begins "Our Father."

The prayer of St. Francis, as a follower of Jesus, is quite similar. Francis taught his brethren his own expanded version of the Lord's Prayer, with themes drawn from Sacred

Scripture. For example, reflecting on "Hallowed be thy name," Francis employed a passage from Ephesians as a framework: that you "may have power to comprehend with all the saints what is the breadth and length and height and depth, and to know the love of Christ" (3:18). Francis comments:

> Holy be Your name.
> May knowledge of You become clearer in us
> that we may know
> the *breadth* of Your blessings,
> the *length* of Your promises,
> the *height* of Your majesty,
> the *depth* of Your judgments.[58]

Francis's rendition of the verse "Your will be done on earth as it is in heaven" refers to the "great commandment" of Jesus (Luke 10:27):

> Your will be done on earth as in heaven
> that we may love You
> *with our whole heart* by always thinking of You,
> *with our whole soul* by always desiring You,
> *with our whole mind* by always directing all our
>   intentions to You,
> and by seeking Your glory in everything,
> *with all our whole strength* by exerting
> all our energies and affection of body and soul
> in the service of Your love and of nothing else;
> and we may love our neighbor as ourselves
> by drawing them all to Your love with our whole
>   strength,
> by rejoicing in the good of others as in our own,
> by suffering with others at their misfortunes,
> *and by giving offense to no one.* (2 Corinthians 6:3)[59]

In an exhortation given to the first group of lay people who, between 1209 and 1215, came to St. Francis wishing to share in his Gospel way of life, Francis expanded upon one of his favorite texts: "For whoever does the will of my Father in heaven is my brother, and sister, and mother" (Matthew 12:50).

> We are spouses when by the Holy Spirit the faithful soul is united to Jesus Christ. We are his brothers when we do the will of his Father who is in heaven. We are mothers to him when we bear him in our heart and in our body through pure love and a clean conscience and we bring him forth by holy work which ought to shine as an example to others.
>
> O how glorious and holy and great to have a Father in heaven! O how holy, fair, and lovable to have a spouse in heaven! O how holy and how beloved, well pleasing and humble, peaceful and sweet and desirable above all to have such a Brother who has laid down his life for his sheep, and who has prayed for us to the Father, saying: [here follows a pastiche of Jesus' "high priestly prayer" to the Father from John 17].[60]

In a later edition of this same exhortation, Francis added another prayer immediately following the above, which acclaims:

> Since he has suffered so many things for us
> and has done and will do so much good to us,
> Let every creature which is in heaven
> and on earth and in the sea and in the depths
> render praise to God
> and glory and honor and blessing;
> for he is our strength and
> power who alone is good,
> alone most high,
> alone almighty and admirable,

glorious,
and alone holy, praiseworthy and blessed
without end forever and ever. Amen.[61]

The prayer of St. Francis of Assisi is fervent, exuberant, and heartfelt. It is shaped by Scripture, especially by the words of Jesus in the Gospels. Francis's prayer is humble before the majesty of God, grateful for all his blessings and the signs of God's goodness (especially in creation), and exultant in proclaiming his glory. Even Francis's "Earlier Rule" — ordering the life of his followers — concludes with extended prayer that ends with an invocation of the saints. He follows that with an exhortation:

Let us all,
everywhere,
in every place,
at every hour,
and at all times,
daily and continually
believe, truly and humbly,
and let us hold in our hearts,
and love, honor, adore, serve,
praise and bless,
glorify and exalt,
magnify and give thanks to
the most High and Supreme Eternal God,
in Trinity and Unity,
to the Father, and Son, and Holy Spirit,
to the Creator of all,
to the Savior of all
who believe and hope in him,
and love him, who,
without beginning or end,
is immutable, invisible,
unerring, ineffable,

incomprehensible, unfathomable,
blessed, praiseworthy,
glorious, exalted,
sublime, most high,
sweet, amiable, lovable,
and always wholly desirable above all forever and
ever.
Amen.[62]

This is what we see when we look through this "window" into the soul of Francis of Assisi. His prayer was pure love and exaltation of God. He desired to live for God and God's glory alone and so incorporated this into the rule of life for his followers. If one lives in this degree of union with and love of God, it seems that all the prescriptions of the rule will follow — or perhaps it is the opposite: all the prescriptions of the rule should lead to this kind of prayer and to this degree of union with God.

A HEART OVERFLOWING WITH PRAISE

St. Francis, "God's Troubadour," wrote two prayers that are similar in form and particularly beautiful and striking. In these "Salutations," he sings the praises of the one most worthy of human praise — God's human mother, Mary — and also praises the most exalted of the Christian virtues.

The Salutation of Mary begins, "Hail, O Lady, Holy Queen, Mary, holy Mother of God, who are Virgin made Church" (the latter is a title unique to St. Francis). The prayer's six-fold salutation ("Hail") of Mary proclaims her as God's palace, tabernacle, dwelling, robe, servant, and mother. The prayer concludes with a greeting that seems to introduce, perhaps as a companion prayer, the Salutation of the Virtues and indicates the source of these virtues as the Holy Spirit:

And hail, all you holy virtues,
Which are poured into the hearts of the faithful
Through the grace and enlightenment of the Holy
    Spirit,
That from being unbelievers,
You may make them faithful to God.[63]

The Salutation of the Virtues praises "Queen Wisdom ... with your sister, holy pure Simplicity," "Lady holy Poverty ... with your sister, holy Humility," and "Lady holy Charity ... with your sister holy Obedience." St. Francis prayed that the Lord would protect each of these who proceed from him. One cannot possess any of these "without dying first," and to offend any of these virtues is to offend all of them.

Each one of these virtues "confounds" all manner of "sin and vice":

- holy Wisdom confounds Satan;

- holy Simplicity confounds the wisdom of the world and of the body;

- holy Poverty confounds the desire for riches and all greed and worldly care;

- holy Humility confounds pride;

- holy Charity confounds every temptation and carnal fear;

- and holy Obedience confounds carnal (fleshly) wishes and "keeps the body mortified to the obedience of the Spirit and to the obedience of one's brother."[64]

Besides these prayers, which could be used anytime, St. Francis also composed liturgical prayers to be used by his brothers as part of or as a supplement to the Liturgy of the Hours. His "Office of the Passion," to be used especially during the sacred Triduum (Holy Thursday to Easter Sunday), is particularly rich. He ended all the Hours with this antiphon to the Blessed Virgin Mary and a concluding prayer, both of which he composed:

> Holy Virgin Mary,
> among the women born into the world,
> there is no one like you.
> Daughter and servant
> of the most high and supreme King
> and of the Father in heaven,
> Mother of our most holy Lord Jesus Christ,
> Spouse of the Holy Spirit,
> Pray for us
> with Saint Michael the Archangel,
> all the powers of heaven
> and all the saints,
> at the side of your most holy beloved Son,
> our Lord and Teacher.
> Glory to the Father, and to the Son, and to the
> Holy Spirit.
> As it was in the beginning, is now, and will be
> forever. Amen.
> Let us bless
> the Lord God living and true!
> Let us always render him
> praise, glory, honor, blessing and every good.
> Amen. Amen.
> So be it. So be it.[65]

Toward the end of his life, St. Francis wrote some of his most memorable and powerful prayers, reflecting the deepening of his own spiritual life as he drew ever closer to Jesus. St. Francis traveled with Brother Leo to Mount LaVerna (Alverno) in 1224, two years before his death. There he was divinely imprinted with the stigmata, the wounds that Jesus bore on his crucified body.

At that time Francis personally wrote praises of God for this great blessing on a parchment he entrusted to Brother Leo, which is preserved to this day in the Basilica of St. Francis in Assisi. Characteristically, the prayer is mainly comprised of a short declaration of who God is:

> You are strong, you are great, you are the Most High, you are King Eternal, you, Holy Father, King of heaven and earth.
>
> You are three in one Lord.... You are Good, all good, Highest good, Lord God living and true.
>
> You are Love, Charity; you are Wisdom, you are humility, you are patience, you are Beauty, you are gentleness; you are security, you are quiet, you are joy; you are our hope and joy, you are justice, you are temperance, you are all our riches.... You are Protector, you are our guard and defender, you are refreshment, you are our sweetness, you are our eternal Life....[66]

On the other side of the parchment, Francis wrote a blessing for Brother Leo that is widely recognized and used today as a "Franciscan blessing."

> May the Lord bless you and keep you,
> May he show his face to you and have mercy on you,
> May he turn his countenance to you and give you peace.[67] (See Numbers 6:24–26.)

Because of its subject, perhaps the most famous and uniquely "Franciscan" prayer of St. Francis is his "Canticle of the Creatures," which he started writing a year or so before his death when he was in great pain, though the prayer radiates joy and thanksgiving. The Lord is praised in and through all his creatures, who are Francis's (and our) "brothers and sisters": Sir Brother Sun, Sister Moon and the stars, Brother

Wind (with the air and every kind of weather), Sister Water and Brother Fire, and our sister Mother Earth. Scholars think that the last two sections of the Canticle were added by St. Francis later.

The section in which God is praised through those who give pardon, bear infirmity and tribulation, and endure in peace referred to the need for reconciliation of warring cities and factions. The final section, added as Francis was close to death, praises the Lord for "our sister Bodily Death." The last verse of the canticle may have been used as a response or refrain after each verse of the Canticle: "Praise and bless my Lord, and give Him thanks and serve him with great humility."[68]

Two of Francis of Assisi's last writings were a "Letter to the Entire Order" (1225–1226) and his "Testament" (1226). In his Testament St. Francis recalls that "the Lord gave me such faith in churches that I would pray with simplicity in this way and say, 'We adore you, Lord Jesus Christ, in all your churches in the whole world, and we bless you, because by your holy cross you have redeemed the world.'"[69] In his Letter to the Entire Order, Francis exhorts all his followers to honor Jesus and his holy name, and especially Jesus present in the holy Eucharist:

> O wonderful loftiness and stupendous dignity!
> O sublime humility!
> O humble sublimity!
> The Lord of the universe,
> God and the Son of God,
> so humbles Himself
> that for our salvation
> He hides Himself
> under an ordinary piece of Bread!
> Brothers, look at the humility of God,
> and pour out your hearts before Him!
> Humble yourselves
> that you may be exalted by Him!

Hold back nothing of yourselves for yourselves,
that you may be exalted by Him!
Hold back nothing of yourselves for yourselves,
that He Who gives Himself totally to you
may receive you totally![70]

There is much to learn from St. Francis about prayer. His prayer is simple and direct. He praises God in Himself, one and triune, and proclaims that God is gloriously praised in his saints, in the virtues he bestows, and in all creation. He recognizes and honors God manifested in his holy name, in churches, and in a special way in the Eucharist. Because Francis was truly humble before God and humanity, his exaltation of the Lord is even more radiantly pure and genuine.

POPE FRANCIS AND PRAYER

We see many of the same qualities in the person and the prayer of Pope Francis. His humility before God became evident even on the night he was introduced as pope, when he asked everyone to pray for him before he imparted his first papal blessing. Cardinal Sean O'Malley, O.F.M. Cap., archbishop of Boston, commented:

> What happened next [after the silent prayer for the pope] was most impressive: he led the people in praying the Our Father, the Hail Mary, and the Glory Be. This was a very moving moment for me because it occurred to me that these very simple prayers are the ones that every Catholic knows, regardless of education and training. People of all ages know these favorite prayers, which unite us as a Catholic people in our life of faith and worship of God.[71]

The decision to lead people in these prayers was very much in the spirit of St. Francis, who not only used the prayers of the Church but also went out to the people to meet them where they were. In this same spirit, Pope Francis has chosen to celebrate daily Mass at the more public Vatican guest house of St. Martha, rather than in the private papal chapel in the Vatican. What occurred on the night Jorge Mario Bergoglio was introduced as the new pope — and asked for prayers — was not an anomaly. He frequently requested, and continues to request, prayers for himself, and prayer is his first response to any need.

On his first morning as pope, Francis rose early and went to pray at the Basilica of St. Mary Major, dedicating the city of Rome and his pontificate to Our Lady. His first papal tweet, reinforcing his focus on prayer, was: "Dear friends, I thank you from my heart and I ask you to continue to pray for me. Pope Francis."[72]

The same man, when archbishop of Buenos Aires, was humble enough to kneel and, overlooking doctrinal differences, receive prayers from Pentecostal preachers during a meeting in Buenos Aires.[73]

Besides asking for prayer for himself, Pope Francis frequently prays publicly for others. He makes it clear that he considers this an essential service he is called to do, especially for the sick and the needy. Two examples, among many, illustrate his commitment. In early October 2013, Mario Palmaro, a bioethicist who worked for Radio Maria, coauthored an essay entitled "We Do Not Like This Pope." Shortly after, when Pope Francis learned that Palmaro had been diagnosed with a debilitating disease, the pope telephoned him. Palmaro later told reporters, "He just wanted to tell me that he was praying for me."[74]

In a general audience on November 6, 2013, the pope asked prayers for a young girl, Noemi, who was suffering from a usually fatal degenerative disease. *L'Osservatore Romano*, the Vatican newspaper, reported:

There was quiet weeping on Wednesday morning at St. Peter's Square. It accompanied a surreal moment of silent prayer led by Pope Francis. He had asked the crowd to join him in "an act of love," a prayer for a little girl who is about to be taken to Heaven. "Her name is Noemi," the pope said. "This morning I went to see her ... the poor little one was smiling.... Let us offer this act of love for her." "We do not know her," but "she is one of us," a Christian, he said....[75]

Obviously the pope cannot pray personally for every ill or needy person, though clearly his desire is to do so. In addition to this concern for the individual, Pope Francis has also called the Church universal to special times of prayer for global needs, such as for the refugees who lost their lives at sea near Lampedusa, Italy, and for their families and loved ones. He also invited Catholics worldwide to an hour of adoration before the Blessed Sacrament on the Feast of Corpus Christi (the Body of Christ) — an idea that reflects St. Francis of Assisi's deep and intense devotion to Jesus in the Eucharist. Pope Francis led this prayer in a simple and unpretentious way, praying silently.

At the beginning of September 2013, the pope called the world to pray for the peaceful resolution of the international crisis concerning the alleged use of chemical warfare in Syria by the government, even against their own civilians.

On September 7 here in St. Peter's Square, from 7 PM [to] 12 AM, we will gather in prayer and in a spirit of penance, invoking God's great gift of peace upon the beloved nation of Syria and upon each situation of conflict and violence around the world. Humanity needs to see these gestures of peace and to hear words of hope and peace! I ask all the local churches, in addition to fasting, to gather to pray for this intention.

Let us ask Mary to help us respond to violence, to conflict and to war with the power of dialogue, reconciliation and love. She is our mother: may she help us find peace. We are all her children. Help us, Mary, to overcome this most difficult moment and to dedicate ourselves each day to building an authentic culture of encounter and peace in every situation. Mary, Queen of Peace, pray for us![76]

The pope then presided over the four-hour prayer vigil. The result? Shortly after, a potentially bloody military confrontation in Syria was averted. Seen through the eyes of faith, this was an answer to prayer. But even after the immediate crisis was averted, Pope Francis continued to call for prayer for peace and religious freedom in the Middle East:

Let us confidently pray that in the Holy Land and in the entire Middle East peace may rise again from the far too frequent and oftentimes dramatic interruptions of the peace process. May enmity and division cease. May peace negotiations which have often been paralyzed by conflicting and dark interests resume quickly. At long last may real guarantees of religious liberty be given for all people, together with the right for Christians to live peacefully where they were born, in the homeland which they have loved for 2,000 years, that they might contribute to the common good as they have always done.[77]

It is evident that for Pope Francis, prayer for the individual needs of others and for the great needs of the world is not a pious sentiment but the first and most essential response of a Christian. Since his election he has spoken of this, but like St. Francis, his own example provides the great est teaching about and witness to its importance. His daily life as pope is steeped in prayer, despite (or rather, because of) the many demands of his office.

Time magazine named Pope Francis "Person of the Year" for 2013, and even the secular journalists who wrote the *Time* article couldn't miss the importance of prayer in Pope Francis's life:

> Francis begins, ends and dots his day with prayer. He rises at 5 a.m. and prays until 7 before celebrating morning Mass at the Casa Santa Marta chapel. He prays after Mass and again before breakfast. Then at 8 a.m. the day begins. He works through papers until 10, then meets with secretaries, cardinals, priests and lay people until noon, followed by lunch and a half-hour siesta.
>
> Six hours of work follow, then dinner and more prayer in front of the Blessed Sacrament. He admits he sometimes nods off at this point, but says, "It is good to fall asleep in God's presence."
>
> He is usually in bed by 10.

Pope Francis has described prayer as a mixture of "courage, humility, and service,"[78] and certainly it takes courage to be persistent in prayer. In a homily in December 2013, Pope Francis recalled Jesus' stories and teachings on prayer: the annoying friend who came in the middle of the night asking for food, the widow who kept coming back to petition the corrupt judge, and the many afflicted with leprosy and other diseases who called or reached out to Jesus for healing.

Pope Francis explained: "Prayer [has] two attitudes: needy and confident. When we ask for something, our prayer is needy … and it is also confident: listen to me [God], I believe you can do it, for you have promised it!" He said that "praying is a little like bothering God so that he listens to us."

It's "drawing God's eyes and heart to us.... Jesus tells us: 'Ask!' and he also says: 'Knock at the door!' and whoever knocks at the door makes noise, he disturbs, he bothers."[79]

Of course, for Pope Francis the prayer of petition is only one aspect of Christian prayer. Like St. Francis, the pope's focus is often on giving praise and thanks to the Lord for who he is and for his goodness, love, and many blessings. The pope's prayer is based firmly on biblical principles, and his spontaneous prayers are marked by a St. Francis–like simplicity. For example, when he recommended praying daily to the Holy Spirit, particularly that we would be open to Jesus, Pope Francis gave us a straightforward prayer that he said we should offer daily: "Holy Spirit, make my heart open to the word of God, make my heart open to goodness, make my heart open to the beauty of God every day." [80]

Pope Francis's gaze is always outward in service, but it is rooted in the inwardness of his relationship with God in prayer. He speaks often about the necessity, for a Christian, of a personal relationship with Jesus Christ and his love and mercy. But the distinctive "inwardness" in the prayer of Pope Francis can also be seen in his call to be a Jesuit and, more so, a Jesuit spiritual director.

A fellow Jesuit who has studied Pope Francis's spirituality indicated that his "first and then recurrent experience as a Jesuit was making and directing the spiritual exercises of St. Ignatius of Loyola, the founder of the Jesuits. Twice at least he has made the thirty-day retreat, and he has also guided others over many years through the experience." One example is a Holy Week retreat based on the Spiritual Exercises given to the bishops of Spain when he was a cardinal.[81] A Jesuit commentator notes that at the heart of this Ignatian spirituality is "a constant preoccupation with the person of Jesus — in his teaching and preaching ... climaxing in prolonged meditation on his death and resurrection."[82]

Pope Francis spoke of the centrality of Jesus, both for the Society of Jesus and for all Christians, when he celebrated the Feast of St. Ignatius of Loyola on July 31, 2013. In his homily, the pope urged each of us to ask the all-important question "Is Christ the center of my life?... [D]o I truly put Christ at the center of my life?" And the way Jesus Christ is placed at the center of our life is through prayer.

At the end of this same homily, Pope Francis recalled the last interview conducted with the long-time Jesuit minister general, Fr. Pedro Arrupe, before he suffered a stroke and began a slow decline to death. Pope Francis recounted that Fr. Arrupe said, "I say this as if it were my swan song: pray." "Prayer," Pope Francis emphasized, is "union with Jesus." This is the priority for a Christian, as it was for St. Francis, as it is for Pope Francis, who humbly implored the whole Church and all people on the evening of his election: "Pray for me."

CHAPTER 4

POVERTY: IN
IMITATION OF JESUS

Some people are confused by what Christians say about poverty. Sometimes poverty is spoken of as an evil or a "curse" that Christians are called to remedy through social justice initiatives and charitable works. The Bible, in both Testaments, condemns those who neglect or oppress the poor and praises those who work to help them. In either case, poverty itself is assumed to be a burden that should be lifted.

What, then, do we make of Pope Francis's statement in a meeting with media correspondents three days after his election, "Oh, how I wish for a Church that is poor and for the poor!" And how do we explain St. Francis of Assisi's "love affair" with "Lady Poverty," which he pursued with such fervor from his conversion to his death?

This apparent conundrum is resolved by considering Jesus, both his person and his teaching. As St. Paul said: "For you know the grace of our Lord Jesus Christ, that though he was rich, yet for your sake he became poor, so that by his poverty you might become rich" (2 Corinthians 8:9). This is the mystery of *kenosis*, the self-emptying of the Son of God (see Philippians 2:7), who voluntarily took "the form of a servant" in order to share all the riches of his grace and redemption.

For the Christian, choosing poverty is all about following and imitating Jesus Christ. St. Francis chose to be poor because Jesus embraced poverty. He wanted to follow as closely as possible the example of Jesus, who said: "Foxes have holes, and birds of the air have nests; but the Son of man has nowhere to lay his head" (Matthew 8:20; Luke 9:58). St. Francis insisted that he and his followers not own houses or property in imitation of the "homeless" Christ, though at times they would build shelters or small dwellings to protect themselves from the elements.[83]

Not only was poverty an imitation of Jesus, it was also a response to his teaching. When Francis of Assisi began to attract followers, he sought the Lord's guidance about how they were to live together as a community. Two of the earliest sources of Francis's life recount that Francis and his first followers went to a local church and prayed that the Lord would give them direction through Sacred Scripture as to how they were to live. Then, opening the missal three times, they came upon three passages from the Gospels:

- "If you would be perfect, go, sell what you possess and give to the poor, and you will have treasure in heaven." (Matthew 19:21)

- "If any man would come after me, let him deny himself and take up his cross and follow me." (Matthew 16:24)

- "Take nothing for your journey, no staff, nor bag, nor bread, nor money; and do not have two tunics." (Luke 9:3)[84]

These texts became the basis for their way of life, and when Francis composed his first rule in 1209 and 1210, the very first chapter began:

> The rule and life of these brothers is this, namely: "to live in obedience in chastity, and without anything of their own, and to follow the teachings and footprints of our Lord Jesus Christ, who says: [Here he quotes Matthew 19:21, Matthew 16:24, Luke 14:26, and Mark 10:29–30, which reads, "Ev-

eryone who has left father or mother, brothers or sisters, wife or children, houses or land because of me, will receive a hundredfold and will possess eternal life."][85]

Clearly, voluntary or "Gospel" poverty is at the heart of God's particular call to St. Francis and his followers. Francis understood that this poverty, freely chosen in imitation of Jesus, was not a curse but a source of blessing. It is not coincidental that the first beatitude taught by Jesus is "Blessed are you poor, for yours is the kingdom of God" (Luke 6:20) (or "poor in spirit" in Matthew 5:3). Jesus warns how difficult it will be for the rich to enter the kingdom of heaven (Mark 10:23–25), illustrating this with the story of a rich man who is condemned for failing to help the poor man on his doorstep, while the poor Lazarus is welcomed into Abraham's bosom (Luke 16:20–25). On the other hand, "Blessed is he who considers the poor" (Psalm 41:1), and to the poor themselves God promises good things (see Psalm 107:9) if they are righteous and trust in God.

THE UNIQUENESS OF ST. FRANCIS'S VIEW OF POVERTY

Building on the Old Testament view that God will reward and vindicate the righteous and bless those who are generous to the poor, Jesus presents poverty as something that can enable one to inherit the kingdom of heaven, if that kingdom is the treasure that one seeks above all. Yet material poverty is difficult in many ways, inducing much bodily and mental suffering. In the Christian tradition, suffering becomes bearable and is even appreciated as something positive when understood to be a sharing in the suffering of Christ. St. Paul was able to say, "Now I rejoice in my sufferings for your sake, and in my flesh I complete what is lacking [that is, still to be completed] in Christ's afflictions for the sake of his body, that is, the Church" (Colossians 1:24). In following this teaching, Christians have been able to rejoice in suffering — even martyrdom — and in the various hardships caused by poverty. In the early Church the monastic movement fostered a life of simplicity and poverty as a means to grow in union with God, particularly by providing freedom from worldly concerns so that followers could devote themselves to prayer.

What is distinctive about St. Francis's view of poverty? First, we can see Francis's noble, chivalrous spirit when he honors Lady Poverty — a personification of this virtue that is uniquely Francis's. In his Salutation of the Virtues, he salutes, "Lady holy Poverty, may the Lord protect you, with your Sister holy Humility."[86] Second, Francis and his followers found joy in being poor. In the account of Francis's conversion by Thomas of Celano (his first *Life of Francis*), Francis heard proclaimed at church the Gospel about the disciples of Jesus carrying no money, staff, shoes, or extra tunic when they went out to proclaim the Good News. After Francis asked the priest to explain this to him, Francis "immediately exulted, saying, 'This is what I want,... this is what I seek, this is what I desire with all my heart.' The holy father, overflowing with joy, hastened to implement the words of salvation."[87] Of Francis's followers, one early account says:

> Although extreme poverty abounded in them, they were always generous, and spontaneously shared the alms given them with all who asked for the love of God.... They rejoiced most in their poverty, for they desired no riches except those of eternity. They never possessed gold or silver, and although they despised all wealth of this world, it was money especially that they trampled underfoot.[88]

Paradoxically, poverty was the great treasure of Francis and his followers. In his last writing, his Testament, St. Francis asked that holy poverty continue to be observed but also reminded his followers to do "honest work," only begging alms when necessary.[89]

There is a third aspect that is distinctive about St. Francis's view of poverty, and here his teaching is very similar to that of Pope Francis. St. Francis wrote in his Earlier Rule:

> Let all the brothers strive to follow the humility and poverty of our Lord Jesus Christ and let them remember that we should have nothing else in the world except, as the Apostle says: *having food and clothing, we are content with these.*
>
> They must rejoice when they live among people considered of little value and looked down upon, among the poor and the powerless, the sick and the lepers, and the beggars by the wayside.
>
> When it is necessary, they may go for alms. Let them not be ashamed, and remember, moreover, that our Lord Jesus Christ, the Son of the all-powerful living God, set His face like flint and was not ashamed. He was poor and a stranger and lived on alms — He, the Blessed Virgin, and His disciples.[90]

Recall that God called Francis in his conversion not just to renounce money or worldly possessions but also to embrace a change of status: he was to become one of the poor, the marginalized, and the outcasts. He was to live among them as a simple poor man, as he often referred to himself. And in his rule, Francis makes it clear that his followers must do the same, and this should be a source of joy.

Pope Francis, as we shall see shortly, is challenging Catholics to go to the outskirts, among the marginalized and the poor — among any who are, as St. Francis said, "considered of little value and looked down upon." The truth is that every person is of inestimable value in God's eyes and never should be looked down upon, regardless of income, race, religion, or physical condition. As archbishop of Buenos Aires, Cardinal Bergoglio lived in an ordinary downtown apartment and took public transportation to work in order to be among the people he was called to serve. As pope he expressed this solidarity with the poor in a symbolic way when he went to a prison and washed the feet of young men and women there in the 2013 Holy Thursday service.

ST. FRANCIS'S POVERTY IN HIS TIME

St. Francis was not the only one in his time to value and pursue poverty. In fact, he and his followers were part of a widespread social phenomenon called the Poverty, or Mendicant, Movement. As Europe became more affluent in the twelfth century, so too did the Church. Large and beautiful Gothic cathedrals were built in the cities, and monasteries grew in wealth. One branch of the Poverty Movement, critical of this growing worldliness, lived a simple life and even preached the Gospel publicly — a right reserved to the clergy — because in their view the diocesan clergy failed to do any of this. These groups were often initially faithful to the Catholic Church but later broke away.

Even more harmful to the Church were groups who viewed the material world as corrupt or evil and preached renunciation of earthly good and mortification of the body as ways of breaking from this evil. They espoused a spiritual life that despised the allurements of the body and the created order. These groups, often labeled *Cathari* (the "pure"), were considered heretical because they saw no good in anything in the created world. For this reason they rejected the idea of a sacrament, a material sign through which God's grace comes to us. Why would God use "evil matter" to impart something pure and good? The Gnostics and the Manichaeans of early Christian history were precursors of these thirteenth-century heretical groups. They too saw the material order as corrupt and therefore to be rejected and despised. St. Francis, on the contrary, gloried in the goodness of God's creation.

There were other Catholics besides St. Francis and his followers who advocated poverty, remained faithful Catholics, and accepted Catholic doctrine on the goodness of creation. Foremost among these were the Spaniard Dominic Guzman and the religious community he founded, the Order of Preachers (the Dominicans). As their name implies, the focus of their ministry was preaching the Gospel, especially to the Cathars in an attempt to bring them back to the Catholic Church.

Before he founded this order, St. Dominic, a diocesan priest, had gone with his bishop to try to convert the Albigensians — Cathars living in the Albi region of southern France. However, the clerics' apparent worldliness, coming on horseback in rich ecclesiastical garb, had been a major obstacle to the extremely poor Albigensians' hearing of their message. Learning from that experience, Dominic founded a community of religious dedicated to living evangelical poverty as part of their witness to the Gospel and the truth of the Catholic Church. Dominic and Francis were "brothers" in living Gospel poverty, as well as in loyalty to the Church.

Even though Francis and his followers sometimes had opportunity to preach the Gospel, their focus was on living a radical life in imitation of Jesus Christ, with poverty as a primary aspect of their witness. St. Francis was led to embrace poverty principally for two reasons. First, he was moved by specific Gospel texts in which Jesus called those who would follow him to sell their possessions and renounce earthly goods. Embracing poverty was, first and foremost, Francis's personal response to a word that he believed Jesus was speaking directly to him. It was what St. Paul calls "the obedience of faith," the only suitable response to God's revelation and call. The Dogmatic Constitution on Divine Revelation (*Dei Verbum*) of the Second Vatican Council explains:

> The "obedience of faith" (Romans 16:26; see Romans 1:5; 2 Corinthians 10:5–6) must be given to God as he reveals himself. By faith man freely commits his entire self to God, making "the full submission of his intellect and will to God who reveals," and willingly assents to the Revelation given by him. (*Dei Verbum*, no. 5)

Living poverty was not, for Francis of Assisi, just an idea he had or something he decided to do because others were doing it in this Poverty Movement. Francis heard particular words of Jesus from the Gospels about discipleship — following Jesus — and he obeyed, in faith, by grace and the help of the Holy Spirit. (*Dei Verbum*, 5, goes on to explain that these are essential.[91])

The second thing that is distinctive about Francis's embrace of Gospel poverty is something I believe Francis discovered more fully as he lived it: this poor life brought him peace and, above all, freedom. For Francis, to live poverty meant to put oneself entirely in God's hands, to trust God completely for everything, like "the birds of the air" and "the lilies of the field" of which Jesus spoke (Matthew 6:25–33; Luke 12:22–31). Perhaps this is why Francis also rejoiced in created things, because in them he recognized not only God's beauty but also his providence: God's faithful care of all that he has made.

This poverty was not deprivation for Francis but a positive thing — an act of trust in God, in which the one who lived poverty would experience the Lord's faithful care and provision. Yes, it was also at times an opportunity to share in the sufferings of the poor Christ, but that, for Francis, was another positive thing. He saw the opportunity to imitate Jesus in his humility and poverty as something noble; it is a privilege to share in the Lord's own chosen way of life.

St. Francis particularly loved those things that reminded him of Jesus' lowliness: Jesus' birth in a stable (a scene Francis reenacted with great joy), his simple life, and his abandonment and suffering as he approached his passion and death. St. Francis was given to see the Lord's presence and face in the poor and marginalized, even in those who had been most repulsive to him, the lepers. The observance of Gospel poverty set Francis free to be at home with the weak, the poor, and the sick, and so this was the lifestyle that he, and his followers, gratefully and joyfully embraced. Most of all, Francis was poor because he loved Jesus and wanted to imitate him in everything.

POPE FRANCIS ON POVERTY

I think it is accurate to say that the primary reason Cardinal Bergoglio took the name Francis after St. Francis of Assisi was because St. Francis's life was the epitome of poverty, a life lived in conscious imitation and following of the poor Christ. As Pope Francis's pontificate unfolds, his concern for the poor and his call for solidarity and personal contact with the poor have been at the forefront of much of his teaching.

In a discussion with students, Pope Francis answered a question with words that could have come just as easily from the mouth of St. Francis of Assisi: "Where do I find hope? In the poor Jesus, Jesus who made himself poor for us."

> Poverty demands that we sow love. It requires me to have greater hope too. Fr. [Pedro] Arrupe … said to all of us, "Look, it is impossible to talk about poverty without having an experience with the poor."… Poverty is the flesh of the poor Jesus. But do not let yourselves be robbed of hope by well-being, by the spirit of well-being that in the end brings you to become a nothing in life…. Where do I find hope? In the flesh of the suffer-

ing Jesus and in the poverty. There is a connection between the two.[92]

Pope Francis bemoans the fact that we have come to accept the millions afflicted with poverty. We take this poverty as a matter of fact and hence do nothing about it. In his talk on the Vigil of Pentecost 2013, Pope Francis observed that when a tramp dies of the cold or when a great many children are lacking sufficient food, we never hear about it because it is not "news." But if the stock market falls slightly, it's on the front page and viewed as a tragedy. Not so when people starve to death or when their health is poor. "This is our crisis today! And the witness of a poor church for the poor goes against this mentality."[93]

What is Pope Francis's solution to the plight of those who are suffering because of poverty and its effects? It appears that his response is threefold. The first two points are very much like St. Francis's approach. First, become poor, or at least poorer, ourselves. In a discussion with young people, Pope Francis said that each of us must consider whether we can be a little poorer ourselves, a little more like Jesus, the "poor teacher." [94]

There is a witness value in the way we live, and living a poorer life is part of that witness. When Pope Francis reflected on how we could become a poor Church, he said:

> I shall return to the idea of witness. First of all, living out the Gospel is the main contribution we can make.... The Church ... is called to make present in society the leaven of the Kingdom of God and she does this primarily with her witness, her witness of brotherly love, of solidarity and of sharing with others.[95]

Second, we must have personal contact with the poor as we assist them, as St. Francis and his followers did. In his 2013 Pentecost Vigil talk, Pope Francis spoke of questions he would sometimes pose in the confessional. He would ask, "Do you give alms?" and if the response was yes,

> I would ask them two further questions: "Tell me, when you give alms, do you look the person in the eye?" "Oh, I don't know, I haven't really thought about it." The second question: "And when you give alms, do you touch the hand of the person you are giving them to or do you toss the coin at him or her?"[96]

I cannot help thinking of St. Francis, whose most profound conversion occurred the moment he could make personal contact with the leper in giving him alms. Pope Francis summarized this call to proclaim "the good news to the poor" (see Luke 4:18) in charity in a message given to the annual ecclesial convention of his diocese of Rome in June 2013:

> The proclamation of the Gospel is destined for the poor first of all, for all those ... who all too often lack what they need in order to live a dignified life. To them first are proclaimed the glad tidings that God loves them with a preferential love and comes to visit them through the charitable works that disciples of Christ do in his name. Go to the poor first of all: this is the priority.[97]

St. Francis of Assisi certainly saw the preferential love for the poor as a priority as well.

The third aspect of Pope Francis's response is one that he is able to carry out in a particular way as pope, representing the Catholic Church to the world in an official way. This is an appeal for the reform of the world's economic and political systems so that the poor are no longer oppressed by perspectives and policies that do not see their welfare as a priority nor even take it into account. Some of his teachings on this world order that idolizes money are certainly consistent with the views of St. Francis, who did not wish his followers even to touch money. This is not feasible as an economic policy, but Francis's life is certainly a witness that calls attention to how easy it is for money (as well as power) to become an idol.

In May 2013, Pope Francis welcomed four new ambassadors to the Holy See. He took the occasion to comment on money and economics on the international level.

> We must … acknowledge that the majority of the men and women of our time continue to live daily in situations of insecurity, with dire consequences. Certain pathologies are increasing, with their psychological consequences; fear and desperation grip the hearts of many people, even in the so-called rich countries; the joy of life is diminishing.…
>
> One cause of this situation, in my opinion, is in our relationship with money, and our acceptance of its power over ourselves and our society. Consequently the financial crisis which we are experiencing makes us forget that its ultimate origin is to be found in a profound human crisis. In the denial of the primacy of human beings!
>
> We have created new idols. The worship of the golden calf of old (see Exodus 32:15–34) has found a new and heartless image in the cult of money and the dictatorship of an economy which is faceless and lacking any truly humane goal.… Money has to serve, not to rule! The Pope loves everyone, rich and poor alike, but the Pope has the duty, in Christ's name, to remind the rich to help the poor, to respect them, to promote them. The Pope appeals for disinterested solidarity and for a return to person-centered ethics in the world of finance and economics.[98]

Cardinal Giovanni Montini (later Pope Paul VI) offered a prayer in Assisi on the Feast of St. Francis, October 4, 1958, in which he asked: "Is friendship between Lady Poverty and Lady Economics possible? Or are we inevitably doomed by the terrible words of Christ: 'It is easier for a camel to go through the eye of a needle than for a rich man to enter the kingdom of God' (Matthew 19:24)?"[99] The lives and teachings of St. Francis and Pope Francis give us hope that there is a solution. The world's economic policies do not seem inclined to embrace or foster Gospel poverty, but the witness of St. Francis and Pope Francis remind us that "with God all things are possible" (Matthew 19:26).

CHAPTER 5

COMMUNION: TOGETHER ON THE JOURNEY

Many well-known Christians had fascinating conversions. St. Paul fell to the ground when a light flashed around him and literally blinded him (see Acts 9:3–4). St. Augustine, hearing the voice of a child singing, "Take and read," picked up a Bible, opened it at random, and read the first passage his eye fell on. He was freed from the bondage of lust, and at that moment his conversion was complete. St. Ignatius of Loyola was converted as he read the life of Christ and the lives of the saints while recovering from a war wound. St. Teresa of Avila one day looked on an image of Jesus scourged and bloody and was convicted of her own infidelity and lukewarmness. And St. Francis of Assisi encountered Jesus Christ when he showed mercy to a leper and when he heard Jesus speak to him as he prayed before the cross of San Damiano.

At these moments God revealed himself and his will to these saints in a direct and personal way. Each of them had been on a spiritual journey that was very individual. Only Teresa of Avila, of those just named, was part of any sort of religious group at the time of conversion, and Teresa's experience with Christ seemed to occur without much influence from her religious community, which was rather lax and permitted its members quite a bit of freedom.

However, after these conversions, each of these figures discovered that conversion to Christ was to be lived out in deep communion with others. St. Paul developed close bonds with many followers of Christ, especially with fellow workers spreading the Good News, such as Barnabas and Timothy. St. Augustine formed a community of Christian philosophers and later, when he became a bishop, wrote a rule for the common life of the priests who shared in his pastoral ministry. St. Ignatius founded the Society of Jesus with the men who joined him after his conversion. Teresa of Avila had a vision for reform of the Carmelite order based on a more Christ-centered, prayerful, and austere community life.

And Francis of Assisi? As we have seen, the young Francis was engaged in a personal quest to discover direction for his own life, and God spoke to him in transforming his revulsion to lepers and in calling him to "rebuild my Church." Initially Francis saw these actions of God's grace as a personal calling, just for himself. Starting a religious movement was not part of Francis's plan when he stripped himself of his clothing and presented himself to Bishop Guido to live as a penitent. But then, as Francis revealed in his Testament, "the Lord gave me some brothers." One by one, others who observed Francis and his humble work sought to join him. Actually, the full text of the passage from Francis reads: "And when God gave me brothers, no one showed me what I should do, but the Most High revealed to me that I should live according to the form of the Holy Gospel."[100]

"No one showed me what I should do" aptly describes what Francis thought when Bernard of Quintaville and another man, Peter Catanii, expressed their desire to join him. As we saw in the last chapter, they embraced four passages from Scripture calling them to a life of utter poverty. Francis felt his way forward from there, but this was the beginning of the Franciscan movement.

THE GROWTH OF THE FRANCISCAN BROTHERHOOD

Even though Francis had some natural leadership qualities that were recognized when his young friends acclaimed him "King of Youth," he had no pastoral formation that equipped him to lead a religious community. His conversion led to a deep compassion for the poor and the outcast and a burning desire to love and serve God totally and unreservedly. His attire was ragged, and his prayer was fervent. Though still mocked and misunderstood by the citizens of Assisi, including his former friends, the sincere witness of his fervor and humility began to stir up the same zeal in others. That was enough for Francis to become a religious founder, though he would have rejected any such title.

Looking back and summarizing what the Lord had called him and his brothers to do, Francis in his Testament speaks of poverty, common prayer, obedience, and manual labor. Those who would follow Francis had to give away all their possessions to the poor except for a few basic items of clothing. If they were clerics, they devoted themselves to praying the Divine Office. (Francis and a couple of the original members had received the tonsure and been ordained to the diaconate in Rome.) Lay brothers prayed simple prayers such as the Our Father. The men were unpretentious, at the service of everyone, and worked with their hands in order to earn, not money, but food and basic necessities and to steer clear of sloth. If no work was available, they would beg alms from door to door.

It is easy to romanticize this life. Obviously, it entailed many hardships. After returning from approval of the first, simple rule by Pope Innocent III, Francis and his followers found shelter in a small abandoned barn about two miles from Assisi at a place known as Rivo Torto. Even though they only stayed there three months, this is considered the first experience of Franciscan common life, lived primarily under the direction and in imitation of Francis.

Francis alone discerned who would join the group, and he began to develop pastoral skills as he got to know each of them personally. He reportedly had to dismiss one brother (whom he called "Brother Fly") who refused to do his share of work or begging. The most memorable story from this period is of a brother who awoke at night groaning and said he was dying — of hunger. Francis, who was at his side, ordered everyone to wake up and to join in a "midnight snack" so that the "dying" brother would not be embarrassed to eat by himself.[101]

As they outgrew the shed at Rivo Torto, Francis looked for a new place for the community to live. At length the Benedictines allowed them to settle by a small abandoned church on the plain near Assisi, a chapel known as St. Mary of the Angels, which Francis called his "little Portion" (*Portiuncula*). This was an answer to prayer because Francis had decided that he and his brothers should live near a church where they could worship together. The Lord provided the Portiuncula, and soon afterward God sent priests to join Francis, men who would celebrate Mass.

Since Francis did not have a plan to attract followers or to form a religious group, what emerged reflected his own call and character. As Augustine Thompson remarks, "Unlike earlier founders, Benedict, Augustine, Bernard — Francis presented his followers, not with a coherent rule, but with himself."[102] His followers lived like Francis, following as literally as possible the teaching and example of Jesus, above all by a poor and humble lifestyle. They were, like Francis, penitents and "minors," little ones with no social status or prestige.

It is characteristic of the early order that when a certain Giles from Assisi went to Rivo Torto to try out this life, he was uncertain until Francis asked him to give his mantle to a poor man who came to them for aid. Giles did so, and this sealed his decision to join Francis as the first "lay" brother. He remained a faithful follower of Francis and was present at the saint's death

By all indications, Francis was a compassionate and merciful father to those who followed him, and he preferred to lead by example rather than by legislation. Both in communal life and in travel, Francis had his followers take turns leading the activities of the house or, when traveling, of the travelers. No one was to be ambitious or greedy for influence. Francis echoed St. Paul's teaching that through love they were to be servants of one another (see Galatians 5:3).

Francis's followers came from all social classes — the rich and the poor — but once they joined Francis they were equal, though possessing different gifts that Francis drew forth and put to use. While some religious communities appeal to people with particular strengths characteristic of the community, followers of St. Francis have always included those with quite diverse backgrounds, gifts, and personality types. Some, like Brother Juniper as portrayed in the *Fioretti (Little Flowers of St. Francis)*, are whimsical, while others are practical and down-to-earth. Some are scholars, while others are not. This is not surprising for the followers of a saint who has such widespread appeal and who strove in his own life simply to imitate Jesus Christ, especially in his poverty and humility.

DEVELOPMENT OF ST. FRANCIS'S RULE

Although Francis would have been content to have his followers live by the Gospel as their rule, focusing on those passages on poverty that the Lord had given him, he dug deeper as he called them to live according to the Gospels and other New Testament writings. "The First [Version of the] Letter to All the Faithful," written sometime between 1210 and 1215, was an exhortation addressed to a group of his first followers. He called them "brothers and sisters of penance." The structure of the document is reminiscent of some of the earliest Christian writings, such as the *Didache* and the Epistle to Barnabas, which have sections contrasting the way of light (that is, living in obedience to God's call) and the way of darkness. Francis contrasts those who, in response to God's grace, do penance and those who refuse to do penance. He lists five characteristics of those who do penance — who are following the way of light:

1. They love the Lord with their whole heart and their neighbor as themselves (Mark 12:30).

2. They hate the sins and vices springing from their bodies.

3. They receive the Eucharist.

4. They bear fruit as they do penance.

5. Those who do these things are "spouses, brothers, and mothers of our Lord Jesus Christ."[103]

Francis says that those who do *not* do these things are liable to judgment and the fire of hell.

St. Francis was not concerned with developing a rule but simply with living the Gospel. He resisted (successfully) having to adopt the rule of any other religious community, but when a rule was mandated, he composed one. He started the document, which reflects many of his core values, in 1209 or 1210, and this early rule was expanded and revised and finally completed by the last general chapter held in Assisi at Pentecost in 1221.[104] The heart of the rule is contained in its first chapter, in which Francis calls his followers to leave everything behind and follow wholeheartedly in the footsteps of Jesus.

This rule, however, intended to be more comprehensive and specific, goes on for twenty-three more short chapters, the longest of which is an extended prayer of praise and thanks to God immediately before the document concludes. What does this rule tell us about Francis's beliefs about communion among his followers? To summarize some key points:

- Brothers who wish to join this fraternity are to be received with kindness and encouragement. After a year of probation, they may join the order and should be obedient to the rule and not be allowed to join another order or to forsake obedience.

- Prayer is the center of Christian life and required of all the brothers according to their state (that is, clerical or lay). Brothers in positions of authority must correct and encourage their brethren in a spirit of service, mindful to treat others as they would want to be treated. The brothers under their authority, in turn, must obey — these matters affect their spiritual well-being. Mutual correction is important. If one brother sees another brother living sinfully, he should correct and help him.

- The brothers must refrain from doing evil to one another and must serve and obey one another in love.

- Brothers are to work in honest professions and look for ways to do good. They must rejoice when they live among people considered of little value and looked down upon — among the poor, the powerless, the sick and the lepers, and the beggars by the wayside.

- When it is necessary, they may go for alms, without shame, remembering that Jesus Christ was not ashamed but was poor and a stranger and lived on alms.

- Each brother should confidently make known his need to another, that the other might discover what is needed and minister to him. Each one should love and care for his brother as a mother loves and cares for her son in those matters in which God has given him the grace. The brothers are to strive to be humble in everything and to avoid delighting in themselves because of their good works or deeds, because all of this comes from God.

In conclusion, Francis stresses that they are all brothers and reminds them of Jesus' words not to call anyone father or teacher, since he is their teacher, and to cling to the Gospel. Finally, at the chapter's climax, Francis quotes almost the entire seventeenth chapter of John's Gospel, in which Jesus exhorts his followers to love each other as he has loved them and to be united, to be one, even as he and the Father are one, so that the world may know that the Father has sent the Son and that they may see the Father's glory in his kingdom.[105]

ST. FRANCIS AND POPE FRANCIS'S VISION OF COMMUNION

St. Francis's powerful Gospel vision of communion is embodied in his life, his teaching, and his rule. It is based firmly on the Gospel of Jesus Christ, who shows us that the way to the Father and to the kingdom of God is through practical, loving communion with others, beginning within our own immediate communities (whether the family, parish, or religious community) but also extending to those outside this sphere, especially the poor and the marginalized.

St. Francis's teaching resonates in the life and teaching of Pope Francis, who also emphasizes that communion is at the heart of God's plan. "What is God's plan?" he asked in a general audience. "It is to make of us all a single family of his children, in which each person feels that God is close and feels loved by him,... feels the warmth of being God's family."[106] Like St. Francis, Pope Francis puts these words into action, frequently reaching out personally to others, as we saw when he embraced and kissed a man severely disfigured by tumors on his head and neck.[107]

Pope Francis also warns against behaviors and sins that undermine communion, just as St. Francis did at certain points of his rule. In chapter 2 of the "Earlier Rule," St. Francis admonishes the brothers to avoid such community-killers as slander, arguments, anger, grumbling, gossip, and judgment, striving instead to love and care for one another in humility.

From early in his pontificate, Pope Francis has similarly denounced sins against charity, especially sins of speech and judgment. He has warned against "gossiping Christians" who have fallen into the habit "of 'flaying' each other alive with words, with misinformation, or with slander. Gossip, the pope said, 'is destructive to the Church.'"[108] In order to preserve harmony, the pope exhorts us to turn to the Holy Spirit:

> In the Church, it is the Holy Spirit who creates harmony. One of the Fathers of the Church has an expression which I love: "The Holy Spirit himself is harmony…." Only the Spirit can awaken diversity, plurality and multiplicity while at the same time building unity.[109]

On the same theme, Pope Francis said:

> In the Church there is variety and a diversity of roles and functions; there is no flat uniformity, but a wealth of gifts that the Holy Spirit distributes. Yet, there is communion and unity: each one relates to the other and comes together to form a single living body, deeply tied to Christ.
>
> Let us remember this well: being part of the Church means being united to Christ and receiving from him the divine life that makes us live as Christians; it means … learning to overcome subjectivism and division, to understand each other

better, to harmonize the variety and the richness
of each person; in a word to love God and the people beside us more, in the family, in the parish, in
associations. Body and limb, in order to live, must
be united![110]

What a beautiful statement of specific ways we can all
build unity! Further, the pope explained, God asks us to leave
behind individualism — the inclination we all have to retreat
into ourselves. "He calls us to be part of His family." Pope
Francis explained that this communion is possible only because we have received the mercy of God, forgiving our sins:
"[W]hen we realize we are sinners we encounter the mercy
of God who always forgives. Never forget it: God always par-
dons and receives us into his love of forgiveness and mercy."[111]

Knowing God's mercy and forgiveness, Christians can
in turn extend God's love to others: "[W]hat is most burdensome in life ... is a lack of love. It weighs upon us never to
receive a smile, not to be welcomed."[112]

In a particularly direct teaching, Pope Francis said
that when people in need approach the Church, the Church
must not close its doors on them simply because their situ-
ations are irregular. He gave the example of a single mother
who wanted to have her child baptized but was turned away
from the parish because she was not married. The pope
commented:

Look at this girl who had had the courage to carry
her pregnancy to term [and not have an abortion].
What does she find? A closed door.... This is not
good pastoral zeal, it distances people from the
Lord and does not open doors. So when we take
this path,... we are not doing good to people, the
People of God. Jesus instituted seven sacraments,
and with this approach we institute the eighth, the
sacrament of the pastoral customs office.

Finally, affirming that Jesus wants everyone to be close to him, Pope Francis urges that we ask the Lord to grant that "all who approach the Church find doors open to encounter Jesus' love."[113]

Pope Francis's inaugural Mass took place on the Feast of St. Joseph, and in his homily he noted the saint's role as a protector — both of the Holy Family and of the Church — and emphasized the need for all people, especially Christians, to imitate St. Joseph. As he explained, being a protector begins by recognizing God's reflection and presence in all of creation and in every person. Certainly this is key to strengthening unity.

> The vocation of being a "protector," however, is not just something involving us Christians alone; it also has a prior dimension which is simply human, involving everyone. It means protecting all creation, the beauty of the created world, as the Book of Genesis tells us and as Saint Francis of Assisi showed us.
>
> It means respecting each of God's creatures and respecting the environment in which we live. It means protecting people, showing loving concern for each and every person, especially children, the elderly, those in need, who are often the last we think about. It means caring for one another in our families: husbands and wives first protect one another, and then, as parents, they care for their children, and children themselves, in time, protect their parents.
>
> It means building sincere friendships in which we protect one another in trust, respect, and goodness.
>
> In the end, everything has been entrusted to our protection, and all of us are responsible for it. Be protectors of God's gifts! Whenever human be-

ings fail to live up to this responsibility, whenever we fail to care for creation and for our brothers and sisters, the way is open to destruction and hearts are hardened.[114]

One expression of Pope Francis's care for others and of raising awareness of our communion with those in dire need was his visit in July 2013 to Lampedusa, an island off the coast of Italy where thousands of immigrants have drowned over the years as they tried to reach safety. The Holy Father commented:

> Today no one in our world feels responsible. We have lost a sense of responsibility for our brothers and sisters.... In this globalized world, we have fallen into globalized indifference. We have become used to the suffering of others.... We are a society which has forgotten how to weep, how to experience compassion — "suffering with" others: the globalization of indifference has taken from us the ability to weep![115]

Some find Pope Francis's criticisms of those who succumb to legalism or indifference rather harsh at times. Perhaps they cannot see how these discomforting corrections reflect compassion for others or even how they reflect the mercy and patience of Jesus. We often overlook Jesus' harsh criticisms of pharisaism — hypocrisy — and of indifference to the plight of the poor, as in his story of the rich man and poor Lazarus at his doorstep (see Luke 16:19–25).

Both Pope Francis and St. Francis point out areas where the faithful occasionally have failed in communion. Remember that St. Francis — a model of compassion — in his role as "pastor" of his order, had to correct or even occasionally expel a brother from their fellowship. In his Earlier Rule he spoke about those who refuse to do penance and are preoccupied by the world, who lack wisdom, who are in the grip of the devil, and who, when they die, will find themselves in anguish as the devil takes them to himself.

It would not be fitting, however, to end a chapter on the importance of communion in following Jesus on a negative note. Pope Francis saw that the tragedy of Lampedusa and others like it present followers of Christ with opportunities to express their care for and their communion with those in need. St. Francis and his followers felt likewise when they reached out to serve the lepers and those on the margins of society. The call for Christians is to show mercy, compassion, and forgiveness to those within the body of believers as well as those in need on the outside.

St. Francis was the first to convict himself of sin against unity and charity. One day a brother in his order brought in a leper to join them at their community meal. St. Francis became irritated and, in a moment of weakness, asked why the brother had done this, since it was not their custom. Immediately, Francis felt convicted of his lack of charity, apologized, and invited the leper to sit next to him. Francis proceeded to eat out of the same bowl with the leper.

We are all challenged, at times, to live in communion with others, following the example of Christ. At the end of his Mass at Lampedusa, where he said strong words about the "globalization of indifference" and our inability to weep over the great suffering of many people, Pope Francis concluded:

> Before imparting my blessing to you, I want to thank you once again, you people of Lampedusa, for the example of love, charity, and hospitality that you have set us and are still setting us. The Bishop said that Lampedusa is a beacon. May this example be a beacon that shines throughout the world, so that people will have the courage to welcome those in search of a better life. Thank you for bearing this witness![116]

May we all make the most of our opportunities to build and express communion with others.

CHAPTER 6

CHURCH: TO LIVE AS CATHOLICS

After exploring the importance of living in communion with others, why do we need a separate discussion of St. Francis's and Pope Francis's understandings of the Church, that is, the Catholic Church? In the case of St. Francis, wouldn't it be enough to simply say that he was a loyal Catholic? And of Pope Francis — well, after all, who is more Catholic than the pope?

If we consider the times in which St. Francis lived, it is by no means a foregone conclusion that someone aspiring to follow Jesus Christ in a radical way would be faithful to the authority and teaching of the Catholic Church. As we have seen, when affluence in Europe increased in the late twelfth century, people began to reflect on Jesus' example and recommendation of poverty for the sake of the kingdom of God. Many felt that this aspect of Gospel living was not evident in the life of the Church and the clergy, nor did clergy always preach the Gospel or even seem to pursue personal holiness.

Clearly, there was need for reform, and various renewal groups began to spring up, usually advocating a return to the simplicity and poverty of Jesus. Some of those groups, like the "Poor Men of Lyons," founded by a rich merchant, Peter Valdes (or Waldo), started well. Valdes, much like St. Francis decades later, gave up his wealth to live a poor, penitential life. His followers, however, soon lashed out, criticizing the clergy for their laxity, and were excommunicated by the archbishop of Lyons. After appealing to the pope, they were reconciled for a time under the conditions that they cease their criticisms and not attempt to interpret Scripture or teach theology. They failed to comply with those norms, and Pope Lucius III condemned the Waldensians in 1184.[117]

The Cathars (from *cathari* — "pure ones") also advocated poverty as a Christian lifestyle and called for reform of Catholic life. They were more widespread than the Waldensians, emerging in the Balkans, Italy, and in what is present-day France.

The Cathars were anticlerical, but what made them even more threatening to the Church was their dualistic belief in the evil of everything material (such as sacraments) and their rejection of the spiritual authority of the Catholic Church. That Church they saw as corrupt and worldly, while they, in their poor austerity, were the "pure ones" — the true, holy (that is, spiritual) Church. On top of this, these Cathars were zealous and evangelistic, and "people admired their austerity and enjoyed their diatribes against the laxity of the clergy."[118]

Young Francis of Assisi could hardly have been unaware of the existence and the teaching of these groups, especially as he and his father must have traveled widely, to France and elsewhere, as cloth merchants. And yet, even though Francis also embraced the call to live in poverty in imitation of the poor Christ, he seems untainted by any critical attitude toward the Catholic Church and her clergy or by any tendency to despise the created order or the sacraments of the Church. To the contrary, Francis expressed in his writing only respect and reverence for everything in the Catholic "order" — priests, sacraments, the Word of God, bishops and the pope, and so on. This is also confirmed almost universally in the accounts about his life. And it doesn't appear to change as Francis's life and ministry unfolded.

From beginning to end, Francis of Assisi was a loyal son of the Catholic Church. The same can be said of Pope Francis, as we will discuss shortly.

EVIDENCE OF ST. FRANCIS'S LOYALTY TO THE CHURCH AND "THINGS CATHOLIC"

For St. Francis, to follow Jesus was to live fully the life of the Church, the Catholic Church. We have already mentioned some of the things Francis did that reflect this: he made a pilgrimage to Rome; he sought advice and support from his bishop, Guido, as he made the decision to live as a penitent; and when he dramatically renounced his worldly possessions, he professed himself beholden solely to "Our Father in heaven" within the Church.

After Francis attracted one or two men who wanted to live as he did, he sensed the need to seek approval for this emerging fraternity from the pope himself. He departed once again for Rome, with his small "band of brothers." This precipitated a debate among the pope's advisers whether to recommend approval of what Francis was doing and of his proposed rule, which was just a collection of Scripture quotations. Considering the problems posed by similar individuals and groups over the previous forty years, it is little wonder that Pope Innocent III hesitated.

Nonetheless, this pope — who called the Fourth Lateran Council and launched the Fourth Crusade, a pope at the apex of the power of the medieval papacy — had the humility, faith, and openness to the Holy Spirit to take the risk of approving a new men's religious community. The pope also incorporated Francis and those who accompanied him to Rome into the Church's structure by having them tonsured and ordained to the diaconate. Francis did not even ask for written approval of his rule or brotherhood, in his humble simplicity. He felt that the pope's word was enough, and so it was until the order began to attract many followers.

That St. Francis was unwaveringly loyal to the Catholic Church and refused to harshly criticize priests and bishops for their shortcomings is clear from his own writings. In his Earlier Rule we see the influence of the Fourth Lateran Council, which condemned the errors of many groups that had broken away from the Church. Clearly, Francis did not want anyone in his order to be numbered among those. Chapter 19 of his Earlier Rule states:

> Let all the brothers be, live, and speak as Catholics. If someone has strayed in word or in deed from Catholic faith and life and has not amended his ways, let him be expelled from our brotherhood. Let us consider all clerics and religious as our masters in all that pertains to the salvation of our souls and does not deviate from our religion [that is, our religious order], and let us respect their order, office, and administration in the Lord.[119]

Even before the Fourth Lateran Council, in his "Earlier Exhortation" to his followers (also known as the first version of the "Letter to the Faithful"), Francis insisted that his followers fast in a Catholic way — that is, not because the body, food, and the material order are evil, as the Cathars and Waldensians held — and that they respect the Church's priests, not because they were sinless but by virtue of their office:

> We must also fast and abstain from vices and sins and from excess of food and drink and be Catholics.
>
> We must also frequently visit churches and venerate and revere the clergy not so much for themselves, if they are sinners, but because of their office and administration of the most holy Body

and Blood of Christ which they sacrifice upon the altar, receive and administer to others.[120]

Perhaps the most eloquent and powerful expression of St. Francis's loyalty to the Church and to all things Catholic is seen in his Testament. Immediately after the opening of the Testament, in which he describes his conversion, and even *before* he speaks of his call to live in simplicity and poverty, Francis speaks of his veneration of churches, priests, the Eucharistic species, anything written bearing a name of God, and even theologians:

> And God inspired me with such faith in his churches that I used to pray with all simplicity, saying: "We adore you, Lord Jesus Christ, in all your churches in the whole world, and we bless you, because by your holy cross you have redeemed the world."
>
> God inspired me, too, and still inspires me with such great faith in priests who live according to the laws of the holy Church of Rome, because of their dignity, that if they persecuted me, I should still be ready to turn to them for aid. And if I were as wise as Solomon and met the poorest priests of the world, I would still refuse to preach against their will in the parishes in which they live. I am determined to reverence, love and honor priests and all others as my superiors. I refuse to consider their sins, because I can see the Son of God in them and they are better than I.
>
> I do this because in this world, I cannot see the most high Son of God with my own eyes, except for his most holy Body and Blood which they receive and they alone administer to others.
>
> Above everything else, I want this most holy Sacrament to be honored and venerated and re-

served in places which are richly ornamented. Whenever I find his most holy name or writings containing his words in an improper place, I make a point of picking them up, and I ask that they be picked up and put aside in a suitable place. We should honor and venerate all theologians, too, and the ministers of God's word, because it is they who give us spirit and life.[121]

We can discern many important things about Francis from this text: his unshakable faith in God's commitment to and action in the Catholic Church; his incarnational faith, that God is present in the Eucharist and acts powerfully through particular places, things, and people; and his humility, his identification as a "little one."

Was St. Francis blind to or naïve about the shortcomings and corruption of priests and the weaknesses of the Catholic Church? This is not the case. Francis acknowledges these, which he would not do if he were unaware of them. Even while Francis charged his followers and others to respect all Catholic priests, he also wrote two "Exhortations to the Clergy," urging them to correct certain abusive or poor practices that he observed among them. The earlier edition of these Exhortations, written before the Fourth Lateran Council (sometime before 1219), begins:

Let us all consider, O clergymen, the great sin and ignorance of which some are guilty regarding the most holy Body and Blood of our Lord Jesus Christ and his most holy name and the written words of consecration.

Then Francis proceeds to chastise clergy who disrespect the sacred mysteries and the Word of God, especially those who administer them "indifferently." He rebukes them for keeping sacred vessels and altar cloths in dirty places and for allowing the Eucharist to be received "unworthily" and administered "indiscriminately." "His names and written words are sometimes trampled underfoot, for the sensual man does not perceive the things that are of God." He reminds the clergy that they will be judged on the basis of these things and urges quick and firm correction.[122]

Notice that St. Francis respected the clergy (priests and bishops) for their God-given authority to celebrate the sacraments and reverently preach the Word of God. His greatest criticism of the clergy was the failure of some of them to carry out these tasks. He did not chastise them for their failure to live exemplary Christian lives; he simply expected them to treat the Eucharist and the Word of God with respect.

Unlike many other reformers of his day, Francis was not a firebrand railing against the many sins of the clergy, nor did he criticize them for not following the standard of poverty he and his followers were called by Christ to live. In the history of Christian renewal and reform movements, this is a very important distinction. Beware the reformer who seeks to make *his* calling and *his* life the standard for the rest of the Church, even for the Church's leaders! St. Francis avoided this because he knew that it was not his place to pass judgment on others (which is different from warning others to avoid sinning and offending God).

Most of all, Francis was truly and genuinely *humble*. We see this in his constant reminders to his followers to be submissive to the Church's ordained leaders, seeing this as God's design for the Church and also knowing himself to be a sinner. (Pope Francis has summarized his own identity as, first, "a sinner."[123])

Further, St. Francis accused himself of his sin and weakness before everyone, from God to all the brothers, saying:

> I have offended in many ways through my grievous fault, especially because I have not observed the Rule which I have promised to the Lord and I have not said the office as prescribed by the Rule

either by reason of my negligence or weakness or because I am ignorant and simple.[124]

Yes, Francis of Assisi believed he knew his place in the Church and in God's plan. He knew he was a sinner and that his salvation would come only through accepting the grace of Christ in a life of penance, prayer, humility, and obedience. It is telling that the very first pledge in the rule of the Franciscan Order is obedience. The prologue of the Earlier Rule promised that Francis and all his followers would obey and revere the pope, and the first chapter of the "Later Rule," issued by Pope Honorius III as a papal bull on November 29, 1223, also highlights obedience to and reverence for the pope.

Poverty is certainly at the heart of St. Francis's way of following Jesus. However, this could not have borne the fruit it did without obedience, which rooted all that Francis and his followers did on a firm, solid foundation. He never wavered from that commitment, and neither have the vast majority of his followers.

You might say that Francis, his order, and the Catholic Church had a beautiful symbiotic relationship based on faith and love, grounded in the communion of the Father, Son, and Holy Spirit. Jesus prayed that his followers would all be perfectly united, even as he and the Father are one (John 17:21). Francis's obedience and fidelity to the Catholic Church and to the Holy Father mirrored Jesus' perfect obedience to his heavenly Father. Of course, St. Francis sought to do the will of God above all, but he understood that this could only be accomplished and bear lasting fruit through his communion with the universal Church, under the guidance of her pastors.

History bears out the truth of this view. Where are the Cathars, the Waldensians, and the Humiliati today, those groups that broke from communion with the Church at the time of Francis of Assisi? Perhaps there are a few small pockets of their descendants remaining, but that is all. And where are the followers of St. Francis, St. Dominic, and the Carmelite order that emerged in the thirteenth century in communion with the Catholic Church? They are everywhere in the world — alive, vibrant, and flourishing where still firmly rooted in obedience to the Catholic Church, her bishops, and the pope.

It should be noted that St. Francis's relationship to the bishops was not servile — he was bold at times in dealing with them. When the cardinal protector of the order, Cardinal Hugolino, suggested that Francis adopt the rule of a preexisting order, he humbly but directly insisted that God had called him to be a new kind of "fool" in the world and that another order's rule would not do.[125]

Francis always sought permission from the bishop to preach when he arrived in a new diocese. One time the bishop of Imola refused his request. Francis persisted, coming back later to ask him again. When the bishop responded irritably, "What do you want now, brother?" Francis answered that when a son is thrown out of his home through one door, he will come back and try to come in through another. The bishop, won over by Francis's humble insistence, embraced him with a smile and granted his request.[126] Francis understood that his filial obedience to the Church was based on a real relationship with those in authority, not just on a theoretical principle.

POPE FRANCIS ON THE CHURCH

One would rightly expect the pope to be faithful and loyal to the Church, and Pope Francis, in his homilies, audiences, and published interviews, uniformly presents the nature and mission of the Church as it is set forth in the teachings of the Second Vatican Council, especially (with regard to the Church's nature) in the Dogmatic Constitution on the Church (*Lumen Gentium*), the council's central document.

There the primary image of the Church is the people of God, and Pope Francis, as we have seen, expounds on this truth that God's plan is to save us as a people, not as isolated individuals. As he said in a general audience in 2013:

> The Church is ... not an organization established by an agreement between a few people, but — as Pope Benedict XVI has so often reminded us — she is a work of God, born precisely from this loving design, which is gradually brought about in history. The Church is born from God's wish to call all people to communion with him, to friendship with him, indeed to share in his own divine life as his sons and daughters....
>
> Still today some say: "Christ yes, the Church no." Like those who say, "I believe in God but not in priests." But it is the Church herself which brings Christ to us and which brings us to God. The Church is the great family of God's children. Of course, she also has human aspects. In those who make up the Church, pastors and faithful, there are shortcomings, imperfections and sins. The Pope has these too — and many of them; but what is beautiful is that when we realize we are sinners we encounter the mercy of God who always forgives. Never forget it: God always pardons and receives us into his love of forgiveness and mercy....

Then, at the end of this audience, Pope Francis posed some questions for us to consider:

> Let us ask ourselves today: how much do I love the Church? Do I pray for her? Do I feel part of the family of the Church? What do I do to ensure that she is a community in which each one feels welcome and understood, feels the mercy and love of God who renews life? Faith is a gift and an act that concerns

us personally, but God calls us to live out our faith together, as a family, as a Church.[127]

So often we hear people say, "I wish the Church would ..." Aren't we, the faithful, the Church? Pope Francis emphasizes, as *Lumen Gentium* taught, that we, the Church, are a people on a journey, a pilgrim people walking together with Jesus.

> I think this is truly the most wonderful experience we can have: to belong to a people walking, journeying through history together with their Lord who walks among us! We are not alone, we do not walk alone. We are part of the one flock of Christ that walks together.[128]

This applies both to those who belong to the Catholic Church — with pope, bishops, priests, religious, and laity all "walking together" — and to the journey of Christians still divided: "We must walk united with our differences: there is no other way to become one. This is the way of Jesus."[129]

Like St. Francis, Pope Francis realizes that the Catholic Church is a church of sinners, of penitents, not a church of the pure and perfect. It is a church of penitents who "allow themselves to be enfolded by the mercy, the tenderness and the forgiveness of the Father, who offers everyone the possibility of meeting him, of journeying toward sanctity."[130]

Pope Francis sees the Church's holiness manifest in the patience and endurance of Christians who strive to do God's will in the ordinary circumstances of everyday life. There are many in the Church who struggle and suffer, and the Church weeps and prays for them, Pope Francis has said, and stands firmly with them. "Our Mother Church has ... the courage of a woman who knows that her children are hers, and that she must defend them and bring them to meet her husband."[131] We hear echoes of St. Francis's care for the members of his order, but in the case of Pope Francis, his care extends to the whole Church, of which he is the chief shepherd.

And here we observe one of the differences between St. Francis and Pope Francis, in spite of the many parallels: they have different calls and responsibilities. St. Francis exhorted — and when necessary even sternly admonished — his brothers to live according to the rule and to be obedient to the Church and her ordained ministers as a visible expression of their obedience to Jesus Christ.

Pope Francis also exhorts and admonishes his brothers — particularly his brother bishops and clergy — challenging them to live the Gospel radically, as he himself tries to do, and to be shepherds who know their sheep by firsthand contact, to be shepherds who have the "odor" of their sheep. He challenges them to show forth the *mercy* of Christ and of the Father as good shepherds, not to turn people off to God's mercy and forgiveness by legalism or bad example.

St. Francis was respectful toward clergy in spite of their weaknesses because he was subject to them as a *minore*. Pope Francis is a peer of the bishops and, as pope, their shepherd, and he is responsible to guide, exhort, and even admonish them. As an archbishop, for example, he did just that. While conducting the Spiritual Exercises of St. Ignatius for some brother bishops, he observed:

> As we read the Gospels, a paradoxical pattern emerges: the Lord is more inclined to warn, correct, and reprimand those who are closest to him — his disciples and Peter in particular — than those who are distant. The Lord acts in this way to make it clear that ministry is a pure grace; it does not depend on the merits or competencies of the one chosen for the mission.[132]

In this conference (and others), he pointed out how the Lord reprimands them (the bishops, including himself) for their failure to live the Gospel fully and faithfully.

Some people have noted that Pope Francis frequently mentions the weaknesses and shortcomings of some of the Church leaders, even in what might be interpreted as a critical tone. In a homily on the parable of the Good Samaritan, he said:

> Now by chance a priest was going down that road. A good priest, in his cassock: good, very good. He saw him [the man beaten and lying on the wayside] and looked: "I'll be late for Mass," and he went on his way. He didn't hear the voice of God there.[133]

In his exhortations and admonishments, the pope is simply exercising his role as head of the Church, calling all to holiness of life and to an energetic living out of the Gospel. Pope Francis's desire for the Church today is that it be seen — and that it operate — more as a community (like St. Francis's followers) than as an institution. As noted previously, to that end he has appointed a group of eight cardinals from around the world to act as his advisers. He is certainly not abolishing the hierarchical structure of the Church, which has its foundation in Jesus' commissioning of the apostles to act in his name, but he's making it more possible for the Church to function in a collegial and transparent manner, with the proclamation and living of the Gospel of Christ as its first and primary priority. And he acknowledges that the Church cannot change overnight, citing the approach to Church governance of Pope St. John XXIII: "See everything; turn a blind eye to much; correct a little." Change takes time.

POPE FRANCIS AS A JESUIT AND A RELIGIOUS

We have been exploring parallels between St. Francis and Pope Francis in following Jesus, but the fact is that, irrespective of his choice of name, Pope Francis is a Jesuit and not a Franciscan. We have seen that St. Francis emphasized obedience to the Catholic Church and her leaders. It should come as no surprise that St. Ignatius of Loyola, founder of the Jesuits, also saw obedience to the Church and to the pope as a foundation for his own spiritual life and later for his religious order.[134]

How does Pope Francis understand this Jesuit value? First, he emphasizes that the Society of Jesus is not focused on itself but on serving Christ and his Church. From the beginning of his pontificate, Pope Francis has stressed repeatedly that every person is called to encounter Jesus as the Son of God and Savior. Our allegiance and obedience are ultimately to him. If one is obedient to the Catholic Church or to one's religious superiors and community, these are expressions of obedience to Jesus Christ and to his Gospel. St. Francis certainly would have agreed.

Another aspect of obedience that shows the originality of Pope Francis is his interpretation of "thinking with the Church." One of St. Ignatius of Loyola's more controversial expressions of obedience is found in his celebrated "Rules for Thinking with the Church": if the Church's *magisterium* declared that black was white and white was black, he would believe it. Although this was an obvious hyperbole stressing the necessity of obedience to and trust in the Church's doctrinal definitions, it has raised questions of intellectual integrity.

Pope Francis, in his exclusive interview with fellow Jesuit Antonio Spadaro, explained that he understood "thinking with the Church" as all members of the Church, as the people of God, listening to each other in the pursuit of truth and what is right. He invokes the concept, found in Vatican II, of the "supernatural sense of the faith of all the people [of God]" — the *sensus fidei (Lumen Gentium*, no. 12, see *Dei Verbum*, no. 8) or *infallibilitas in credendo* — and explains: "This is what I understand today as the 'thinking with the Church' of which St. Ignatius speaks. When the dialogue among the people and the bishops and the pope goes down this road and is genuine, then it is assisted by the Holy Spirit."

His point is that "the Church" is not just the people, or the bishops, or theologians, or the faithful *alone*, but all together they comprise the one people of God. To "think with the Church" (and hence to obey the Church) is to be in true dialogue and communion with each other. Pope Francis clarifies that he does not mean that the "infallibility" of all the faithful is a form of populism or popular vote but rather that it arises when the pastors and people are listening to God together.[135]

He also said that the element of Jesuit spirituality that is most helpful in his ministry as a bishop and as pope is discernment of God's will, seeking to see and hear things from God's point of view. Pope Francis, as a bishop and as pope, especially needs the gift of discernment to distinguish the value and validity of the many "voices" of our time. St. Francis, in his role, was most attentive to the voice of the Lord directing him and his brothers in a unique "prophetic" way. As Pope Francis has said,

> Religious men and women are prophets.... They are those who have chosen a following of Jesus that imitates his life in obedience to the Father; [in] poverty, community life and chastity.... A religious must never give up prophecy. This does not mean opposing the hierarchical part of the Church, although the prophetic function and the hierarchical structure do not coincide.[136]

Pope Francis is aptly describing himself when he says that a religious must not give up prophecy. What is most surprising in the early stages of the pontificate of Pope Francis is that we have a religious as pope who is unabashedly prophetic — who is not afraid to speak a clear, direct prophetic word, not only to the world and to the "average" Catholic but also to the hierarchy of the Catholic Church. To his episcopal and clerical colleagues and brothers he is issuing a challenge to consider how they (and he, as pope) must live and proclaim the Gospel of Jesus more fully and faithfully in this period of history.

Like St. Francis, Pope Francis loves and is passionately committed to the Church but is not afraid to proclaim this prophetic word and to live a prophetic life that challenges everyone in the Church to reexamine how they are doing in following Jesus and living his Gospel, just as St. Francis did so powerfully and effectively in his times.

CHAPTER 7

MISSION: PROCLAIMING THE GOSPEL

When it comes to mission, St. Francis of Assisi and Pope Francis have a very similar, if not identical, understanding. What does *mission* mean? Jesus told his followers to go out and proclaim the "good news" (gospel), which was that the kingdom of God was at hand (see Mark 1:15; Matthew 4:17). After Jesus died and rose from the dead, he sent his Holy Spirit at Pentecost to empower the newborn Church to carry out this mission. The Church did so by proclaiming the death and resurrection of Jesus and the fact that Jesus is "the Christ," the Messiah, the long-awaited Savior of Israel and of all people.

St. Francis and Pope Francis not only agree on this fundamental mission, but both also make clear that this good news of Jesus and his kingdom is something that each person is invited to accept personally through faith.

When Pope Francis went to Assisi on the Feast of St. Francis, October 4, 2013, he said:

> What does Saint Francis's witness tell us today? What does he have to say to us, not merely with words — that is easy enough — but by his life? The first thing he tells us is this: that being a Christian means having *a living relationship with the per-*

son of Jesus; it means putting on Christ, being con-
formed to him.

Where did Francis's journey to Christ begin?
It began with *the gaze of the crucified Jesus.* With
letting Jesus look at us at the very moment that he
gives his life for us and draws us to himself. Francis experienced this in a special way in the church
of San Damiano, as he prayed before the cross....
Jesus' eyes are not closed but open, wide open:
he looks at us in a way that touches our hearts....
When we let the crucified Jesus gaze upon us, we
are re-created, we become "a new creation."

Everything else starts with this: the experience of transforming grace, the experience of being
loved for no merits of our own, in spite of our being sinners. That is why Saint Francis could say with
Saint Paul: "Far be it from me to glory except in the
cross of our Lord Jesus Christ" (*Galatians* 6:14).

We turn to you, Francis, and we ask you:
Teach us to remain before the cross, to let the crucified Christ gaze upon us, to let ourselves be forgiven, and recreated by his love.[137]

The fundamental mission of the Church is to introduce
others to the person of Jesus so that all might become "new
creations" through faith in him. As Pope Francis said on Pentecost 2013, which was also World Mission Day:

The Second Vatican Council emphasized in a special way how the missionary task, that of broaden-
ing the boundaries of faith, belongs to every baptized person and all Christian communities....

Each community is therefore challenged, and
invited to make its own, the mandate entrusted by
Jesus to the Apostles, to be his "witnesses in Jeru-
salem, throughout Judea and Samaria and to the

ends of the earth" (*Acts* 1:8), and this, not as a secondary aspect of Christian life, but as its essential aspect: we are all invited to walk the streets of the world with our brothers and sisters, proclaiming and witnessing to our faith in Christ and making ourselves heralds of his Gospel....

The Church — I repeat once again — is not a relief organization, an enterprise or an NGO, but a community of people, animated by the Holy Spirit, who have lived and are living the wonder of the encounter with Jesus Christ and want to share this experience of deep joy, the message of salvation that the Lord gave us. It is the Holy Spirit who guides the Church in this path. [138]

Could Pope Francis have described the primary mission of the Church any more clearly? In his pontificate he has continued the focus on evangelization as the primary mission of the Church, as taught by the Second Vatican Council and emphasized by his immediate predecessors.

St. Francis of Assisi also sparked a similar "new evangelization" in his own time. His native land and most of Europe were Catholic, but Francis believed that a deeper conversion to Christ and practice of the faith were needed. This sprang from his own personal experience with Jesus and the call he received to live a more committed, even radical Christian life. As we have seen, the little ripple created by Francis's life in the pool of thirteenth-century Western society eventually swelled to a virtual tidal wave.

One might ask, did St. Francis understand proclaiming the Gospel of Christ as a central priority? Wasn't his life more about being an example of Christlike poverty, peace, and joy? It is true that the Scripture passages that St. Francis and his followers brought to Pope Innocent III for approval as the foundation of his rule were passages about following Jesus after giving up one's possessions and leaving "father and mother, brothers and sisters, houses and lands." He didn't come to the pope, for example, with the Great Commission as his rule: "Go therefore and make disciples of all nations" (Matthew 28:19).

To put it another way, it doesn't seem that the young Francis intended his group to be a missionary order or apostolate. But in a prophetic manner, Pope Innocent not only approved Francis's rule but also commissioned him and his followers to preach, as long as they obtained permission from the local pastor or bishop. Augustine Thompson, O.P., explains that when the pope told Francis to go and "preach penance to all" (as Thomas Celano reported),

> This was not quite the commission Francis was expecting.... The pope thought of them as a group of lay preachers.... In sending them off to preach, Innocent did something other than merely approve their intention to give up all things, take up the Cross, and follow Christ. In style of life, he assimilated them to the various lay preaching groups he had been approving for some ten years. It was, for the brothers, a wholly unexpected development. [139]

Pope Francis often alludes to those elusive (perhaps apocryphal) words of St. Francis: "Preach the Gospel; use words when necessary." Even after this commission by Pope Innocent, it appears that Francis and his followers "preached" more by their lifestyle of poverty and care for the sick than by giving sermons. However, Thompson observes that at times St. Francis did preach, in a rather unconventional way, and that this eventually increased his notoriety:

> Francis was always more a man of actions and gestures than of carefully crafted words. Indeed it was his delivery and his persona that most affected his hearers, rather than the words he spoke.... Francis was also known for the enthusiasm with which

he addressed crowds, occasionally dancing and
even breaking into song,... but he might even end
up in tears over the ultimate gift of God, his Son's
death on the cross.... [In] his last sermon to the
nuns of San Damiano ... Francis recited the penitential psalm, the Miserere, sat on the ground and
sprinkled ashes on his head. Doing penance made
a better sermon than talking about it.

Preaching brought with it a greater exposure,
and for a man with Francis's magnetism and attractive personality,..., his reputation for holiness
and access to God [through prophecy] began to
spread. Francis did not encourage the growth of
any cult, but once an audience had been created,
he lost control of his public persona.[140]

Pope Francis's informal speaking style and his occa-
sional prophetic gestures in reaching out to people reflect St.
Francis in some ways. Also, the topic that St. Francis preached
on most frequently was repentance — turning back to God
with sorrow for sin. His first followers identified themselves
as "penitents from Assisi." When Francis preached in Bolo-
gna in 1222, a man recalled that though his sermon topic
was demons and angels, Francis managed to bring the topic
around to repentance and urged his listeners to practice penance — something the angels couldn't do but his listeners,
having bodies, could.[141] Because Francis did not see his followers primarily as preachers, he composed for them exhortations on repentance that any brother could give at any time.
One example, included in the Earlier Rule, proclaims:

Do penance, performing worthy fruits of penance,
because we shall soon die.... Confess all your sins.
Blessed are those who die in penance, for they
shall be in the Kingdom of Heaven. Woe to those
who do not die in penance as they shall go into

everlasting fire. Beware of and abstain from every evil and persevere in good till the end.[142]

Also, in his "First Letter to the Custodians" (1220), Francis wrote to those overseeing the brothers: "In every sermon you give, remind people about penance and that no one can be saved unless he receives the most holy Body and Blood of the Lord."[143] It is clear that St. Francis took seriously the pope's mandate to preach penance, even though preaching sermons was not God's primary call to Francis and his followers.

THE MISSION OF POPE FRANCIS

Of course, Pope Francis has a different office in the Church and lives in a different era than St. Francis. According to the Second Vatican Council, among the duties of bishops, "preaching the Gospel has pride of place" and is always discussed first among his duties.[144] Pope Francis emphasizes that his primary role and identity in the Church's structure is that of a bishop. Hence, he also sees calling the faithful to holiness as his central mission — through his preaching but first through his example.

For Pope Francis, like St. Francis, repentance is a central theme of his preaching. He has been very direct in pointing out specific sins that endanger Catholics and others in our era. It is true that Pope Francis calls attention especially to the mercy of God, yet this mercy and forgiveness only come if one approaches God with a repentant heart, confessing one's sins specifically and turning away from them.

In a homily on the sacrament of reconciliation, Pope Francis explained the reason that Catholics confess sins to another person in this sacrament. Some people say they confess directly to God, "but it's [too] easy; it's like confessing by e-mail." He stresses the need to be sincere and concrete (specific) in confessing sins and even speaks of shame for sin as a "grace," because we should be ashamed of our sins before the sanctity of God, as Peter was when he said, "Depart from me, Lord, for I am a sinful man" (Luke 5:8).[145]

What is the mission of the Church? To bring people to salvation through repentance and faith in Jesus Christ, which comes through the preaching of the Gospel. We see this beginning at Pentecost, when St. Peter gave the first proclamation of Jesus' death and resurrection and called for those who heard to repent, believe, and be baptized. So the call to penance (repentance from sin and a penitential life) is a common focus for St. Francis and Pope Francis, leading people into the way of discipleship, which is the way of the cross.

ST. FRANCIS'S MISSION TO THE SULTAN

In the midst of the Crusader era, Francis of Assisi had a passionate desire for the conversion of Islamic people to Christ — not by threats or force of arms but by the peaceful proclamation of the Gospel. He was a "throwback" to the early Church in his desire for martyrdom if he were unable to convert the sultan. Of course, in the end Francis was granted neither wish, but as always it is his example, the witness of his life, that speaks powerfully about being a follower of Christ.

St. Francis understood clearly that the Church is missionary "by its very nature" — it exists to evangelize.[146] Almost as soon as he began to attract followers, he sent them out to proclaim the Gospel of Jesus Christ in simple terms, beginning with the call to reject sin and turn to God. St. Francis had a mission-oriented outlook from the very start of his new life as a penitent and preacher. His earlier attempts to evangelize outside of Italy had been thwarted because of Cardinal Hugolino's concern that Francis's order would be left without leadership. Francis made sure that interim leaders were put in place before he departed for Muslim-controlled lands.

His mission to the sultan is a long story in itself, but the outcome was that Francis and a companion were brought before the Sultan Malik al-Kamil (1180–1238) near Damietta, Egypt, and they proclaimed the Gospel of Jesus Christ to him. Francis risked offering his life in a trial of faith with the sultan's religious advisers, as Elijah had done with the prophets of Baal. The sultan's advisers called for the execution of Francis and his companion for attempting to convert the sultan to a "false religion," but because Francis never spoke against Muhammad, the tolerant Al-Kamil spared his life and even offered Francis gifts (which he refused, except food) before releasing him.

Thompson believes that Francis was granted such a cordial and extended audience because the sultan believed that Francis must have been sent with some political offer to negotiate. When he was finally convinced that Francis only had religious interests, he released him.[147]

St. Francis might be seen today as a precursor of modern interreligious dialogue, but this would not be entirely accurate. He assuredly did listen patiently while the Muslim religious scholars presented their faith, but Francis saw his mission as simply to proclaim the Gospel in order that his hearers would believe and be saved. The sultan seemed most impressed that Francis was willing to die for his beliefs and that he was respectful and a man of peace.

Pope Francis has exhibited the same peaceful respect in his dialogues with other religious leaders and with the nonreligious and antireligious. His observations about the peace that is evident in the life of St. Francis underscores this attitude that is so critical to the proclamation of the Gospel.

> The peace of Saint Francis is the peace of Christ, and it is found by those who "take up" their "yoke," namely, Christ's commandment: Love one another as I have loved you (see John 13:34; 15:12). This yoke cannot be borne with arrogance, presump-

tion or pride, but only with meekness and humbleness of heart.

We turn to you, Francis, and we ask you: Teach us to be "instruments of peace," of that peace which has its source in God, the peace which Jesus has brought us.[148]

THE MISSION OF COMPASSION AND MERCY

To this point, the focus of this chapter has been the proclamation of the Gospel by St. Francis and Pope Francis by word, supported by the example of their lives. But what is distinctive about the ministries of the saint and the pope? It is not their preaching but their concern for personal, compassionate contact with individuals, especially the poor, the sick, and the marginalized. It is a mission and ministry of "presence" and of example that depends on the witness of their lives more than their words.

One is struck, when considering St. Francis and Pope Francis, by their humility and simplicity, and by their joy. St. Francis was focused not so much on what he and his followers did in their "apostolate," as long as they were spending time generously with the Lord in prayer and were being faithful as brothers (or sisters) to loving and serving each other in their own community.

Pope Francis underscores the need for Christians, including Church leaders, to reach out in real, practical ways to those on the outskirts, those who are marginalized in any way in society or in the Church. This is certainly a key theme in the pontificate of Francis. In his first general audience he said:

> ... [F]ollowing Jesus means learning how to come out of ourselves — reach out to others, to go to

the outskirts of existence, to be the first to move towards our brothers and sisters, especially those who are more distant, those who are forgotten, those who are most in need of understanding, consolation and help. There is so much need to bring the living presence of Jesus, merciful and full of love!

We think of Jesus reaching out to the Samaritan woman at the well, to the Syro-Phoenician woman, to the centurion whose servant was dying, to the widow at Nain whose son had died, to despised tax collectors, to lepers, and to many known to be sinners. Pope Francis's reflections in his first general audience apply not only to Jesus but in many ways to St. Francis of Assisi:

He spoke to everyone, without distinction, to the great and the lowly; to the rich young man and the poor widow, the powerful and the weak; He brought the mercy and forgiveness of God to all; He healed, comforted, understood, gave hope; He led all to the presence of God, who is interested in every man and woman, like a good father and a good mother is interested in each child.

God did not wait for us to go to Him, but He moved towards us, without calculation, without measure. This is how God is: He is always first, He moves towards us.[149]

In his interview in *America* magazine, Pope Francis said that the Church ministers must be "ministers of mercy above all,... people who can warm the hearts of people, who walk through the dark night with them, who know how to dialogue and to descend themselves into their people's night, into the darkness, but without getting lost."[150] One of Pope Francis's favorite images for this is walking. He said:

It is one of my favorite words when I think about a Christian and about the Church...: to belong to a people walking, journeying through history together with their Lord who walks among us. We are not alone, we do not walk alone. We are part of the one flock of Christ that walks together.

But the most important thing is to walk together by working together, by helping one another, by asking forgiveness, by acknowledging one's mistakes and asking for forgiveness, and also by accepting the apologies of others by forgiving — how important this is![5]

In an age when most people travel by car, bus, plane, or train (and some, much fewer, by bicycle), the image of walking may seem anachronistic. In some ways it hearkens back to the time of St. Francis, who walked the hills and roads of Umbria and beyond, as did his followers, meeting people on the way. Nonetheless, the image of walking with another person remains a powerful reminder about slowing down and taking time for personal interaction, which is exactly what Pope Francis wants to promote.

A VISIT TO ASSISI

How could we learn about the relationship of Pope Francis with St. Francis more clearly than in considering the pope's visit to Assisi? Indeed, many of the themes of the pontificate of Pope Francis and the life of his namesake, St. Francis, coalesced and were proposed by Pope Francis during his visit to Assisi on the great saint's feast day, October 4, 2013. Many popes have visited Assisi since Francis's canonization in 1228 (eighteen previous popes), but none have had the name of the Poverello.

Pope Francis's itinerary and talks that day spoke eloquently about his understanding of the Church's mission and how it played out in the life of St. Francis. The pope began his day with a visit to the Serafico Institute, dedicated to the care of sick children and named, of course, after the "seraphic" saint. In his prepared address he recalled St. Francis's meeting with the leper, which changed Francis's life and began his mission to the sick and the poor.

This moment "made him [St. Francis] understand what truly mattered in life: not wealth, nor power of weapons, nor earthly glory, but humility, mercy and forgiveness." In this address Pope Francis called for a "culture of acceptance" of those who are weak and in need, who bear the "wounds of Jesus." He challenged us to "put the most disadvantaged people at the center of social and political attention!"[152]

Several times during the day, Pope Francis took time for personal prayer and meditation, including at the church of San Damiano; at the Basilica of St. Clare before the original San Damiano cross, which is now kept there; and at the tomb of St. Francis in the basilica. Pope Francis, by example, showed the importance of prayer, even during a very busy day. He also visited the "Room of Renunciation," where St. Francis renounced his earthly goods before Bishop Guido and publicly dedicated himself to God's service. Capturing the spirit of that gesture by St. Francis, Pope Francis said:

> We are all called to be poor, to strip us of ourselves; and to do this we must learn how to be with the poor, to share with those who lack basic necessities, to touch the flesh of Christ! The Christian is not one who speaks about the poor, no! He is one who encounters them, who looks them in the eye, who touches them.
>
> I am not here to "make news" but to indicate this is the Christian path, the path St. Francis followed. St. Bonaventure, speaking of the renunciation of St. Francis, writes: "Thus, then, the servant

of the Most High King was left despoiled that he might follow the Lord whom he loved."[153]

After a simple lunch with the poor, Pope Francis addressed a group of young people from the region, touching on some key themes of his understanding of the mission of the Church today. First he spoke about vocations, noting that one great challenge to all vocations today is the "culture of the temporary" — the fear of making a permanent commitment that might not work out. The pope said "not to be afraid to take definitive steps" and pointed out that the Holy Spirit is always providing new answers to new needs.

Then Pope Francis spoke of the vocation that Jesus lived — that of virginity for the sake of the kingdom of God. He stressed that this vocation is not a *no* to marriage but a *yes* to God's call, the same call that Sts. Francis and Clare embraced and that young people around the world continue to choose.[154]

PROCLAIMING THE GOSPEL

With mention of the Gospel, Pope Francis launched into an impassioned and lively response to two questions posed by the young people at Assisi concerning our social obligation and our responsibility to evangelize.

Here in Assisi, close to the Portiuncola, I seem to hear the voice of St. Francis repeating: "The Gospel, the Gospel!" He says it to me as well; indeed, he says it to me first: Pope Francis, be a servant of the Gospel! If I do not succeed in being a servant of the Gospel, my life is worth nothing!

However, dear friends, the Gospel does not only concern religion. It concerns man, the whole of man; it concerns the world, society and human civilization. The Gospel is God's message of salvation for mankind.

When we say "message of salvation," this is not simply a way of speaking, these are not mere words or empty words like so many today…. Mankind truly needs to be saved!

Here Pope Francis joins St. Francis and the whole tradition of the Catholic Church in affirming that the mission of the Church is a continuation of the mission of Jesus to save the human race. From what? From sin and evil. For what? For life with God in his eternal kingdom. How? As Pope Francis continued, through the action of God, who in his infinite mercy has vanquished evil and won the victory through the death and rising of Jesus.

This mission, which begins within each person, must reach out to others. Pope Francis highlighted this:

The Gospel, then, this message of salvation, has two destinations that are connected: the first, to awaken faith, and this is evangelization; the second, to transform the world according to God's plan, and this is the Christian animation of society. But these are not two separate things, they form one mission: to carry the Gospel by the witness of our lives in order to transform the world! This is the way: to bring the Gospel by the witness of our lives.

Let us look to Francis: he did both of these things, through the power of the one Gospel. Francis made faith grow and he renewed the Church, and at the same time he renewed society, he made it more fraternal, but he always did it with the Gospel and by his witness…. Young people of Umbria: you must also do something! Today, in the name of St. Francis, I say to you: I have neither gold nor

silver to give you, but something far more pre
cious, the Gospel of Jesus. Go forward with courage! With the Gospel in heart and hands, be witnesses of faith by your lives: bring Christ into your
home, preach him among your friends, welcome
and serve him in the poor. Young, give Umbria a
message of life, peace and hope! You can do it![155]

Where does the Church find the power and courage
to carry out its mission? In an early general audience Pope
Francis identified the Holy Spirit as the one who equips us
to evangelize.

Evangelizing is the Church's mission. It is not the mission of only a few, but it is mine, yours and our mission. The
Apostle Paul exclaimed: "Woe to me if I do not preach the
Gospel!" (1 Corinthians 9:16). We must all be evangelizers,
especially with our life! Paul VI stressed that "Evangelizing is
... the grace and vocation proper to the Church, her deepest
identity. She exists in order to evangelize" (Apostolic Exhortation *Evangelii Nuntiandi*, no. 14).

Who is the real driving force of evangelization in our
life and in the Church? Paul VI wrote clearly: "... [I]t is the
Holy Spirit who today, just as at the beginning of the Church,
acts in every evangelizer who allows himself to be possessed
and led by him. The Holy Spirit places on his lips the words
which he could not find by himself, and at the same time
the Holy Spirit predisposes the soul of the hearer to be open
and receptive to the Good News and to the Kingdom being
proclaimed" (*Evangelii Nuntiandi*, no. 75). And Pope Francis
affirms:

To evangelize, therefore, it is necessary to open
ourselves once again to the horizon of God's Spirit, without being afraid of what he asks us or of
where he leads us. Let us entrust ourselves to him!
He will enable us to live out and bear witness to

our faith, and will illuminate the hearts of those we meet.[156]

Pope Francis then proceeded to describe three aspects of the Holy Spirit's action in evangelization — aspects that we also see in the life of St. Francis. The first is openness to God through the love of the Spirit, which leads to openness to others, overcoming "closure, indifference, division," and conflict. Ask yourself this, the pope says: "How do I let myself be guided by the Holy Spirit in such a way that my life and my witness of faith is both unity and communion?"

The second element that the Holy Spirit provides is courage, as we see in St. Peter and the apostles on the day of Pentecost and in St. Francis after he first showed mercy to the leper.

The third element is prayer. The Church must ask for "the fire of the Holy Spirit" and build "an intense relationship with God" if it hopes to go out from the safety of its walls and proclaim the Gospel in plain speech.[157]

Pope Francis's vision of mission, like that of St. Francis, is totally God-centered and relies on the grace and guidance of the Holy Spirit. We also see in Pope Francis and St. Francis a beautiful and quintessentially Catholic synthesis of the mission of evangelization — leading others to faith in Jesus Christ as Lord — and the call to minister to the pressing human needs of others, both by charitable works and by seeking to change the world's structures that oppose God's law and true human welfare.

Every Catholic, every person, has a mission from God. Pope Francis challenges each person to prayerfully discover that particular mission and fulfill it by God's grace.

CHAPTER 8

JOY: HALLMARK OF THE CHRISTIAN

The third Sunday of Advent is known as *Gaudete* — or *Rejoice* — Sunday, a word taken from the entrance prayer of the liturgical celebration, reminding us that the birth of the Savior draws near. On Gaudete Sunday of 2013, Pope Francis encouraged the faithful to remember that "the Church is not a refuge for sad people but rather a house of joy." The reason? "Jesus Christ is our joy! His faithful love is inexhaustible!"[158] Driving home the importance of joy as a central Christian characteristic, Pope Francis devoted his first papal apostolic exhortation, released in November 2013, to the joy of the Gospel.

But why is it so important to speak about joy? First, nothing attracts like joy. As Pope Francis understands, nothing can lead others to Jesus Christ, or at least to consider faith in God, as effectively as Christians who are genuinely joyful. Second, this topic is especially important in a book about St. Francis and Pope Francis because joy is a hallmark of their lives — they exude it even more than they speak about it. Isn't St. Francis's joy one of the secrets of his appeal and popularity? He lived a life of severe penance and self-denial, admitting, near his death, how poorly he had treated "Brother Ass," his body. And yet his penances never turned him into a gloomy ascetic. In fact, G.K. Chesterton noted, "The whole point about St. Francis of Assisi is that he certainly was ascetical and he certainly was not gloomy."[159]

St. Francis believed that the only thing that should cause a person to be sad is sin, and the remedy for sin is close at hand — repentance.

> So the Father (Francis) used to censure those who went about with gloomy faces, and once rebuked a friar who appeared with a gloomy face, saying, "Why are you making an outward display of grief and sorrow for your sin? This sorrow is between God and yourself alone. So pray Him in His mercy to pardon you and restore to your soul the joy of His salvation, of which the guilt of your sins has deprived it. Always do your best to be cheerful when you are with me and the other brethren; it is not right for a servant of God to show a sad and gloomy face to his bride, or anyone else."[160]

What else did Pope Francis say on Gaudete Sunday? As described in one news report, his words bear striking resemblance to the advice of St. Francis:

> Encouraging those who feel they can't have a fresh start in life because of their sins, the Holy Father said that God awaits all with mercy and love, ready to forgive. This allows us to overcome sadness and gives us true joy in times of trial. The Pope went on to say that when a Christian is sad, it means that they have distanced themselves from Jesus. The Holy Father stressed the importance of praying for those who are sad and [making] them "feel the warmth of the community."[161]

St. Francis included an admonition to joy in his Earlier Rule, instructing his brothers to avoid the hypocrisy of a gloomy, sad appearance and to conduct themselves instead with cheerful demeanor.[162]

This, of course, was St. Francis's habitual outlook. A notable instance of his joy even in the midst of trial occurred one day when he was walking through a forest singing, in French, the praise of God. Thieves pounced on him, and when they asked him who he was, he said with spirit that he was "the herald of the Great King." The robbers beat him up and dumped him in a snow-filled ditch, saying, "Lie there, you stupid herald of God!" When they left, Francis jumped up out of the snow, and "exhilarated with great joy, he began in a loud voice to make the woods resound with praises to the Creator of all."[163]

This account is reminiscent of the incident in the Acts of the Apostles when Peter and the apostles were beaten for proclaiming Jesus, yet "they left the presence of the council, rejoicing that they were counted worthy to suffer dishonor for the name" (Acts 5:41). The joy that comes from following and obeying Jesus enables the Christian to endure suffering and persecution. In fact, one of the classic stories of St. Francis is his discussion with Brother Leo about what is perfect joy for the Christian, dramatically recounted in the *Little Flowers of St. Francis.*

After Francis first piqued Brother Leo's curiosity by telling him that perfect joy is *not* attained by a friar minor healing all illnesses, driving out all demonic powers, knowing all the mysteries of nature and all the teaching of Sacred Scripture, or even converting all unbelievers, the amazed Brother Leo asked where, then, he would find perfect joy.

St. Francis proceeded to explain, in a similarly dramatic fashion, that if they were to return to the Portiuncula in the midst of rain and freezing cold, and instead of letting them in, the brothers did not recognize them and insulted them, beat them mercilessly with a knotty club, and rolled them in the mud and snow — if they endured all this patiently and without anger for the love of Christ, "Oh, Brother Leo, write: that is perfect joy!"[164]

Like St. Paul, Francis desired not to glory in anything save the cross of our Lord Jesus Christ (Galatians 6:14). To sum it all up: for St. Francis the only joy is found in Jesus, both to suffer for him and to praise him for who he is and for all his gifts. Chesterton spoke of the spiritual life of a mystic (and St. Francis was certainly one) in these words:

> ... [I]n some sense he is there when the foundations of the world are laid, with the morning stars singing together and the sons of God shouting for joy. That is but a distant adumbration [foreshadowing] of why the Franciscan, ragged, penniless, homeless and apparently hopeless, did indeed come forth singing such songs as might come from the stars of morning; and shouting, a son of God.[165]

Those embroiled in the great struggles of the world or even in the ordinary struggles of daily life might find it difficult to understand how we can praise God and rejoice in those trying circumstances. St. Francis knew that this was not only possible but proper and even necessary, because the reality is that Jesus is present in all circumstances and is truly Lord. Therefore he could "rejoice always," as St. Paul urges (1 Thessalonians 5:16 and Philippians 4:4). However, it must be acknowledged that even St. Francis endured times of trial that robbed him of his accustomed joy. Omer Englebert speaks of Francis's great trial of witnessing his own order diverging from his ideal of poverty:

> "Poor little man," said our Lord to him, "why are you so sad? Is not your Order My Order? Is it not I who am its Chief Shepherd? Cease to be afflicted then, and take care rather of your own salvation."
>
> To this man stumbling in the night, distressed at no longer knowing God's will, these words brought back the light. And when, there-

after, the friars came to speak of books, of mitiga
tions of the Rule, and of practice of the older Or-
ders, he would only say: "Do what you will. I am
no longer obligated to do anything except pray for
my friars and give them a good example."

Biographers relate the way in which this "great temptation" ended. One day in the Portiuncula when the saint was
praying in tears, crushed by the weight of his responsibility
and grief, a voice was heard:

> "Francis, if you had faith like a grain of mustard
> seed, you would say to this mountain, 'Be re-
> moved' and it would obey you."
> "What mountain, Lord?" asked Francis.
> "The mountain of thy temptation," contin-
> ued the voice.
> "Lord," replied Francis, "let it be done to me
> according to Your word." And at once the tempta-
> tion vanished.
> Thereafter the conscience of the Little Poor
> Man was limpid and calm once more like a fair
> lake, and a great peace again filled his soul.[166]

Despite this "dark night," St. Francis perhaps more than
any other saint understood and lived what St. Augustine
taught: that humanity is created to praise God and in that
will find true joy. Many are familiar with the saying of Augustine in the beginning of his *Confessions*: "You have made
us for yourself, and our heart is restless until it rests in you."
Fewer know the context of this saying. The first paragraph of
St. Augustine's *Confessions* declares:

> You are great, Lord, and highly to be praised
> (Psalm 47:2): great is your power and your wis-
> dom is immeasurable (Psalm 146:5). Man, a lit-
> tle piece of your creation, desires to praise you,

a human being "bearing his mortality with him" (2 Corinthians 4:10), carrying with him the witness of his sin and the witness that you "resist the proud" (1 Peter 5:5).

Nevertheless, to praise you is the desire of man, a little piece of your creation. You stir man to take pleasure in praising you, because you have made us for yourself, and our heart is restless until it rests in you.[167]

POPE FRANCIS AND JOY: PRE-PAPAL TEACHING

I have heard it said that in Pope Francis's writings before he became pope, the word *joy* and the call for Christians to be joyful in the Lord and in their faith occur more frequently than any other word or theme of his teaching. There are far too many examples to recount from Cardinal Bergoglio's years as archbishop of Buenos Aires, but it's hard not to be moved by his insistence on this fruit of the Spirit.

On the Feast of St. Cajetan in 2011 — St. Cajetan is one of the most popular saints in Argentine culture — the cardinal delivered a homily centered on the Gospel reading about Zacchaeus (Luke 19:1–10).

According to the Gospel reading, Zacchaeus immediately came down from the tree he had climbed and joyfully welcomed Jesus into his house.

This joy *began* as soon as Zacchaeus went out into the street. It *grew* within him as he climbed down from the tree. It *accompanied* him all the time he was preparing his house. It *burst forth* when Jesus entered his house. And it *was strengthened* when he publicly professed that he had decided to change his life....

When Zacchaeus felt his heart bursting with joy with the Master sitting there in his house and could contain it no more, he stood up and publicly declared that he had decided to change his life. It was a decision motivated by joy — not by any external force. Jesus did not say, "You have to change your life." He simply went to visit him at his home. That was enough for Zacchaeus to know what he had to do. It's what Jesus does in the Eucharist. He simply says to us, "I want to visit you in your heart. I ask you to receive me in the Eucharist."[168]

To catechists, in 2012, Cardinal Bergoglio wrote: "Today, more than ever, the act of believing must project joy.... Joy is the doorway through which we announce the Good News and the consequence of living in faith." [169]

In his Chrism Mass homily in 2011, he encouraged his priests to carry out their ministry in a spirit of joy and consolation:

> When there is joy in the heart of the pastor, it is a sign that his actions come from the Spirit. When there is joy in the people, it is a sign that what is reaching them — as a gift and proclamation — is of the Spirit. For the Spirit is a spirit of consolation, not bitterness.

On the other hand, Cardinal Bergoglio pointed out, when there is "a spirit of sour and gloomy *acedia*" (the opposite of our Lord's spirit of consolation), it is like vinegar, which

> ... tries to rob us of the *joy of the present:* the *poor joy* of one who is content with what our Lord gives him each day, the *fraternal joy* of one who enjoys sharing what he has, the *patient joy* of simple, hidden service, the *hopeful joy* of letting oneself be led

by our Lord in today's Church. When Jesus says, "Today this scripture has been fulfilled in your hearing," it is an invitation to the joy and consolations of God's "today."

A final encouragement to the priests is that when they have given joy and consolation to their people in their ministry, they receive it back even more abundantly.

> … [W]hen it comes to joy, what we stand to receive surpasses what we have to give. How our faithful people rejoice when they see that they can give joy to us! How happy they are when we rejoice with them! This is simply because they need pastors who are themselves comforted, who allow themselves to be consoled so that they lead not in complaint or anxiety but in praise and serenity; not in a state of tension but in the patience that comes with the anointing of the Spirit.[170]

Finally, in his *Corpus Christi* homily in 2011, Cardinal Bergoglio proclaimed to all: "Sadness is an evil proper to a worldly spirit. The remedy is *joy*: the joy that only the Spirit of Jesus gives, a joy that nothing and nobody can snatch away." The joy of Jesus, he explains, is first the "joy of forgiveness." It is a joy that comes from experiencing the risen Lord: "The joy of Jesus' presence is always 'catching.'"

It is also a joy we experience when we gather as a community to share in his great gift of the Eucharist, in the presence of our mother, Mary:

> The joy of being companions at the table with the Risen One! When we allow the Spirit to gather us together at the table of the altar, his joy will enter deeply into our hearts, and the fruits of unity and esteem among brothers and sisters will blossom spontaneously in a thousand creative ways.… The

Eucharist is a font of unity. Let us eat this bread, so that we don't end up dispersed, anarchic, split into a thousand competing sub groups.

Let us ask Mary to guard us against the plague of dispersion and contempt: these are the bitter fruits of sad hearts. Let's ask our Mother, the Cause of our Joy,... to help us to savor the bread of the Covenant, the Body of her Son....[171]

POPE FRANCIS AND JOY: PAPAL TEACHING

Jorge Bergoglio chose the name Francis for many reasons, but evidently the joy that marked St. Francis of Assisi was one characteristic that resonated with him and certainly radiates from him in his pastoral ministry In his *first general* papal homily — on Palm Sunday, March 24, 2013 — Pope Francis began by speaking about joy and its source: meeting Jesus Christ and following him.

> And here [is] the first word that I wish to say to you: *joy!* Do not be men and women of sadness: a Christian can never be sad! Never give way to discouragement! Ours is not a joy born of having many possessions, but from having encountered a Person: Jesus, in our midst; it is born from knowing that with him we are never alone, even at difficult moments, even when our life's journey comes up against problems and obstacles that seem insurmountable, and there are so many of them!
>
> And in this moment the enemy, the devil, comes, often disguised as an angel, and slyly speaks his word to us. Do not listen to him!
>
> Let us follow Jesus! We accompany, we follow Jesus, but above all we know that he accompanies

us and carries us on his shoulders. This is our joy, this is the hope that we must bring to this world.[172]

Jesus himself was a man of joy, setting us an example that is reflected in both St. Francis and Pope Francis. Pope Francis has commented that we aren't used to thinking about Jesus smiling or joyful, but "Jesus was full of joy" because of his intimacy with his Father.

> His inner joy comes precisely from this relationship with the Father in the Holy Spirit. And this is the joy he gives to us, and this joy is true peace. It is not a static, quiet, tranquil peace: Christian peace is a joyful peace, for Jesus is joyful, God is joyful.[173]

Jesus is the reason for the Christian's joy. The "author" of this joy, Pope Francis says, is the Holy Spirit. St. Paul lists joy as the second fruit of the Holy Spirit, right after love (Galatians 5:22). This fruit of the Spirit, evident in St. Francis, frees us from sadness and depression. Joy is also the result of praising God, which St. Augustine taught is humanity's deepest desire. The Holy Spirit sets us free to praise God, and this enables the fruit of joy to grow in our hearts.

This is seen in an exemplary way in the life of Mary the Mother of God, whose "Magnificat" is a model prayer of praise and thanksgiving, as her "spirit rejoices in God" her Savior (Luke 1:47). Pope Francis tied all of these themes together in his homily for the Feast of the Visitation on May 31, 2013:

> We Christians are not very used to talking about joy, about happiness. I think that we often prefer complaints! What is joy? The key to understanding this joy is in the words of the Gospel: "Elizabeth was filled with the Holy Spirit."...
>
> It is the Spirit himself who guides us. He is the author of joy, the creator of joy, and this joy

that is in the Holy Spirit gives us true Christian freedom. Without joy we Christians cannot become free. We are enslaved to our sorrows. [The great Pope Paul VI said,] "It is impossible to carry the Gospel any further with sad, dejected, disheartened Christians. It is impossible." This is a somewhat funereal attitude.[174]

As St. Francis had a deep devotion to Our Lady, Pope Francis too expresses the need to pray to Mary for the gift of joy and the grace to praise God. He concluded the Visitation homily with the exhortation:

> It is she, the Virgin Mary, who brings joy. We must pray to Our Lady that in bringing Jesus, she give us the grace of joy, of freedom, the grace of praise. That she give us the grace of praising freely ... for he is worthy of praise for ever.[175]

Not long after, when he went to Brazil for World Youth Day, Pope Francis made a pilgrimage to the National Shrine of Our Lady of Aparecida and there renewed his personal consecration to Mary, the Cause of our Joy.

In his call to joy, Pope Francis appears to be, like St. Francis, a "troubadour for the Lord." He is acutely aware that all the talk and teaching regarding the "new evangelization" will be in vain unless Christians are joyful about their faith and go out living and proclaiming it joyfully. Consider some excerpts on joy from Pope Francis's homilies and addresses:

> Joy is a gift from God. It fills us from within. It is like an anointing of the Spirit. And this joy is the certainty that Jesus is with us and with the Father... Sometimes these melancholy Christian faces have more in common with pickled peppers than the joy of having a beautiful life.

> Joy cannot be held at heel: it must be let go.
> Joy is a pilgrim virtue....[176]

> Far from sorrow, far from simple fun ... it is something else. [Joy] is a grace we must seek.[177]

And though joy is not simple fun, in a later homily based on the Pharisees' complaint that Jesus' disciples ate and drank while others fasted, Pope Francis said that meeting Christ is like going to a wedding — a feast. And so Christians live with joy because life with Jesus "is a great feast."

He continued, saying that Jesus worked a miracle at a wedding when his mother Mary realized that there was no more wine — and without wine, there is no party. "Can we imagine ending a wedding feast with tea or fruit juice? It doesn't work ... it is a feast. And so Our Lady asks for a miracle." This "approach with joy, joyful with all your heart" — this is the life of a Christian.

Of course, Pope Francis added, "there are moments of the cross, moments of sorrow, but there is always that deep sense of peace. Why? The Christian life is ... the wedding feast of Jesus and the Church."[178]

In July 2013, Pope Francis met with seminarians, novices in religious communities, and those discerning religious life. Not unexpectedly, the Holy Father spoke at length about the joy that should accompany the call to priesthood or religious consecration:

> I would like to say a word to you, and that word is joy. Wherever there are consecrated persons, seminarians, women and men religious, young people, there is joy, there is always joy.... Don't be afraid to show the joy of having answered the Lord's call, of the choice to love and witness His Gospel in the service of the Church. And joy, real joy, is contagious; it infects,... it makes us go forward.[179]

Pope Francis went on to discuss the reasons why some priests and religious lack the joy of the Lord. He stressed that there is no holiness in sadness, referring to St. Teresa of Avila's saying, "A sad saint is a sorry saint." Pope Francis observed that the vow of celibacy could lead some to sadness if it did not mature toward "pastoral paternity" or "pastoral maternity" — giving spiritual life to others. But when we see "so many nuns, so many priests who are joyful, it's because they are fruitful, they give life, life, life. They give this life because they find it in Jesus! In the joy of Jesus! Joy, not sadness, pastoral fruitfulness!"[180]

Here Pope Francis warns against hypocrisy and pharisaism. Joy must be authentic, flowing from a consistent Christian life. Poverty, which is a hallmark of consecrated life, must be a genuine and coherent part of that life. Earlier in this address, the Holy Father, in a most Franciscan fashion, noted that true joy cannot be found in possessions or any other worldly standard. An authentic Christian life finds joy only in the Lord, as St. Francis discovered.

AN EXAMINATION OF CONSCIENCE AND A MISSION OF JOY

Pope Francis, in the first months of his pontificate, did not hesitate to challenge and convict Catholics, calling the Catholic Church and all its members to examine their lives in light of the Gospel of Christ. This segment from his Wednesday Catechesis of June 26, 2013, is a prime example of this:

> I would now like us to ask ourselves: how do we live our being Church? Are we living stones or are we, as it were, stones that are weary, bored or indifferent? Have you ever noticed how grim it is to see a tired, bored and indifferent Christian? A Christian like that is all wrong, the Christian must be alive, rejoicing in being Christian; he or she

must live this beauty of belonging to the People of God which is the Church.

Do we open ourselves to the action of the Holy Spirit, to be an active part of our communities, or do we withdraw into ourselves, saying, "I have so much to do, it isn't my job!"?[181]

At the same time, Pope Francis just as consistently has offered encouragement and hope. Where is joy to be found? In the very activity that the last four popes — Pope Paul VI to Pope Francis — have called all Catholics to embrace: evangelization.

Here it is fitting to turn briefly to Pope Francis's apostolic exhortation *The Joy of the Gospel* (*Evangelii Gaudium*, indicated below as *EG*). The first three sections, the document's introduction, explore the meaning of Gospel joy in our time, beginning with the first sentence: "The joy of the Gospel fills the hearts and lives of all who encounter Jesus." This joy in finding Jesus is the reason we evangelize. We are simply sharing our joy as Christians. Yet the first section of this introductory section explains why this joy is thwarted or obscured: "the great danger in today's world" to this joy is "consumerism" that leads to self-absorption (*EG*, no. 2). What is the pope's response to this?

> I invite all Christians, everywhere, at this very moment, to a renewed personal encounter with Jesus Christ, or at least an openness to letting him encounter them; I ask all of you to do this unfailingly each day. No one should think that this invitation is not meant for him or her, since "no one is excluded from the joy brought by the Lord."[182]

If we are ashamed or afraid to come to the Lord (or to come back to him, if we have sinned or just drifted away), Pope Francis explains that we need only turn to Jesus for mercy and forgiveness, because "he has forgiven us seventy times seven.... With a tenderness that never disappoints, but is always capable of restoring our joy, he makes it possible for us to lift up our heads and to start anew" (*EG*, no. 3).

In the next two articles, Pope Francis reviews the Old Testament and New Testament texts on God's call to joy and rejoicing, but he also realizes that yielding to joy is sometimes difficult, and it may be overshadowed with grief and sorrow, as even St. Francis experienced in his times of temptation and challenges within his order. Pope Francis writes:

> I realize of course that joy is not expressed in the same way at all times in life, especially at moments of great difficulty. Joy adapts and changes, but it always endures, even as a flicker of light born of our personal certainty that, when everything is said and done, we are infinitely loved.
>
> I understand the grief of people who have to endure great suffering, yet slowly but surely we all have to let the joy of faith slowly revive as a quiet yet firm trust, even amid the greatest distress: "My soul is bereft of peace; I have forgotten what happiness is.... [B]ut I call this to mind, and therefore I have hope: the steadfast love of the Lord never ceases, his mercies never come to an end; they are new every morning. Great is your faithfulness.... It is good that one should wait quietly for the salvation of the Lord" (Lamentations 3:17, 21–23, 26). (*EG*, no. 6)

The pope recalls that some of the most beautiful expressions of joy he has witnessed are by "poor people who had little to hold on to" and "by others, who even amid pressing professional obligations, were able to preserve, in detachment and simplicity, a heart full of faith" (*EG*, no. 7).

The second section of the introduction to *The Joy of the Gospel* takes its title from a line in Pope Paul VI's great (in

Pope Francis's estimation) apostolic exhortation *Evangelization in the Modern World*. The title is "The Delightful and Comforting Joy of Evangelization." Few Catholics, in my experience, view evangelization as either delightful or comforting, at least not if they're the ones being called to do it.

How can it be seen in the way the pope describes? Pope Francis sees evangelization as sharing the joy of knowing Jesus Christ. St. Francis and his followers shared that joy simply by the way they lived. (And if your life were so full of Gospel joy, people might be *asking* you, "Why are you so happy?") Perhaps we are troubled, either because of what people will think of us if we speak of Christ or because we don't think our words or witness will have any effect (that is, we fear failure). Pope Francis reminds us, however, that evangelization is first and foremost a work of God

At the close of the introduction, Pope Francis says that in the rest of the exhortation he wishes to expand upon "a definite style of evangelization which I ask you to adopt *in every activity which you undertake*. In this way, we can take up amid our daily efforts the Biblical exhortation: 'Rejoice in the Lord always; again I will say, Rejoice' (Philippians 4:4)" (*EG*, no. 18).

He explains further that the joy that filled "the disciples is a missionary joy" (*EG*, no. 21). The particular theme of missionary joy through reliance on the Holy Spirit is especially addressed in chapter 5 of the exhortation, "Spirit-Filled Evangelizers." This final, climactic chapter of the exhortation ties together the themes of mission and joy, especially as reflected in the teaching of Pope Francis and the life of St. Francis.

Given that evangelization is the great challenge and opportunity for Catholics in the present day, to speak of evangelization — of joyful mission — is a fitting conclusion to this chapter exploring how St. Francis and Pope Francis have responded to their call to *live* the Gospel joyfully and to proclaim it boldly with joy. Pope Francis summed up the spirit behind this call — which is given to all of us, not just to popes and saints — in a catechesis delivered in May 2013.

This is another effect of the Holy Spirit's action: the courage to proclaim the newness of the Gospel of Jesus to all, confidently, (with parrhesia) in a loud voice, in every time and in every place.

Today too this happens for the Church and for each one of us: the fire of Pentecost, from the action of the Holy Spirit, releases an ever new energy for mission, new ways in which to proclaim the message of salvation, new courage for evangelizing. Let us never close ourselves to this action!…

Evangelizing, proclaiming Jesus, gives us joy. Instead, egoism makes us bitter, sad, and depresses us. Evangelizing uplifts us.[183]

CHAPTER 9

THE PROFOUND
UN-THEOLOGIAN

This seemingly contradictory chapter title points to the surprising and mysterious paradox of a person who had little or no formal education in theology yet who grasped, taught, and lived the deepest mysteries of the Catholic faith in a way that was truly astounding and that decisively shaped the face and direction of the Church. The person, of course, is St. Francis of Assisi. The image that best captures his impact is the famous fresco in the upper church of the Basilica of St. Francis, portraying Pope Innocent III's dream of a small tattered man dressed in brown, supporting on his shoulder the imposing but teetering Basilica of St. John Lateran, representing the Catholic Church. Pope Francis is the modern-day pope who had no dream about Francis of Assisi but who so appreciated his importance for the Church today that he assumed his name.

Let's review what we have seen about St. Francis so far. Francis of Assisi was an ordinary and, by his own admission, sinful man who heard the message of the Gospel and tried to live it literally and wholeheartedly. The words of Jesus to his followers to leave everything and follow him were words Francis heard addressed personally to him. The words he heard Jesus speaking to him in prayer one day in San Damiano, to "rebuild my Church," were likewise a direct invitation, calling for a personal and specific response. Francis had already left behind the world of luxury and the glory of military exploits. The Lord had freed him from his deepest fears: his revulsion toward lepers and his fear of becoming deformed himself. All that Francis had come to desire was to know and to do the Lord's will, which was his desire as he knelt before the crucifix in San Damiano.

Hearing Francis's prayer, the Lord began to use him to rebuild his Church, one step at a time. First, God sent him brothers — one-by-one — to share his simple way of life. Francis sought approval for this group and the guidance of the Catholic Church, first through his bishop and then, boldly, by going to Rome to seek the approval of the pope. Francis was humble before those Church authorities, indeed toward all priests and bishops, as he was before God. Obedience and fidelity, to God and to "Mother Church," were principles that guided him till his death. Although Francis and his followers were often mocked, misunderstood, and even persecuted, especially in the early years, Francis saw this as sharing in the suffering of Jesus, and he was given the grace to avoid anger and bitterness.

Francis and his followers were controversial at times, but they were not divisive. Francis understood the Gospel sayings about "turning the other cheek," "shaking the dust from his feet" when unwelcome, and freely giving away his clothing to anyone in need, as he and his brothers often did (Matthew 5:39–40; 10:14). Francis insisted that the brothers support themselves by work, but they were not ashamed to beg for food when the need arose, and they even saw begging on behalf of the brothers as a privilege.[184]

In short, Francis and his followers learned about the Gospel and Christian life not primarily through study (except for Sacred Scripture and the Church's prayer) but by striving to *live* it, every day and in every circumstance.

FRANCIS THE UN-THEOLOGIAN

All of his pursuit of Gospel simplicity, poverty, and humility still does not explain one thing. In my estimation, Francis of Assisi — without the benefit of any significant theological education — possessed and communicated a lively and profound grasp of the most essential mysteries of the Christian faith. Of his education, one Franciscan scholar wrote: "Francis possessed no special training. He never went to seminary, never took any religion courses, was never ordained a priest. He was an ordinary, average Christian who one day heard in church the word of the Gospel and let it penetrate into his heart."[185] Francis was one of the simple who was made wise by God's word (Psalm 19:7); one of those "little ones" in whom Jesus rejoiced because the Father had revealed to them the mysteries of the kingdom hidden from the wise and understanding (Matthew 11:25).

Despite his lack of theological education, Francis did not fall prey to any of the heresies and schismatic excesses that were springing up all over Europe among well-meaning visionaries and self-proclaimed Church reformers. Avoiding these could be explained in part by Francis's unwavering loyalty to the teaching and the hierarchy of the Catholic Church. Francis's "reform" was not directed toward criticizing or seeking to correct abuses or weaknesses in the Church. Francis focused on his *own* need for repentance and ongoing conversion, and he taught his followers to do the same. Francis kept busy removing the beam from his own eyes, rather than trying to remove the "specks" in the eyes of his fellow Catholics (Matthew 7:3–5), though he encouraged his brothers to support each other in their penitential quest to follow Jesus in holiness.

Loyalty to the Catholic Church and living a simple, zealous Gospel life, however, do not account for the understanding Francis of Assisi had of the central mysteries of Christian faith. What are these mysteries, and how did Francis reveal his understanding of them? The three that stand out most clearly are *creation*, the *Incarnation*, and *redemption* — that is, the suffering of Christ on the cross, which is the gateway to his glory in the Resurrection, the Ascension, the sending of the Holy Spirit, and his return at the end of time.

Creation

In the midst of the medieval resurgence of the ancient Gnostic and Manichaean dualism, which viewed the whole material order as the work of an evil power or god, Francis delighted without restraint or reservation in the goodness and beauty of the universe as God's creation, the creation of the God who "saw everything that he had made, and behold, it was very good" (Genesis 1:31). No other saint has seen so clearly that "the heavens are telling the glory of God; and the firmament proclaims his handiwork" (Psalm 19:1).

It becomes difficult to distinguish fact from legend in the stories of St. Francis preaching to the larks or taming the wolf of Gubbio, but the truth of Francis's "trademark" love of the created order is indisputably confirmed in his "Canticle of the Creatures." In this exultant poetic prayer, God is praised and glorified in every created thing, which Francis considered his own brothers (sun, wind, fire) and sisters (the moon and stars, water, Mother Earth, and even bodily death). Though Francis loved churches and labored to repair them, he often was drawn to pray in caves on mountainsides or in any isolated spot outdoors, as was Jesus, his master.

If Francis were *only* remembered as the saint of nature or the saint of creation (which he is), he would still have a special place in the hearts of many people. Many of these same people may find his harsh, ascetical life disturbing or at least dissonant with his childlike delight in nature. For Francis, there was no such tension. He saw God's beauty and grandeur in everything created, even when Brother Fire was used to cauterize his eyes toward his life's end, and Brother Wind bit harshly into his meagerly clothed body. Even death, whose sting has been removed by Jesus' death and resurrection, has become a sister with a place in God's plan that gives him glory.

Incarnation

If St. Francis is known for his love of nature, he delighted even more in the apex and crown of that creation, when God joined himself irrevocably with his creation in the person of Jesus of Nazareth, the incarnate Word of God. Francis was overwhelmed with wonder at the humility of God, who condescended to be born of Mary in a stable full of animals and laid in their feeding trough as his first bed, with shepherds coming from the fields to witness his arrival. This was St. Francis's favorite feast day, and he originated the reenactment of the events surrounding Jesus' birth with the first "Christmas play" at Greccio, complete with actors and animals at the crèche or manger scene. Francis wept for joy when the birth of Christ was reenacted.

Again, it appears that Francis's appreciation of the incarnation of the Word of God — the basis for understanding the inherent goodness of the created order — was something that he understood through reflection and prayer, rather than through theological study. It was a matter of the heart more than the head, based on the truth about Jesus that Francis found in Scripture and in Catholic tradition.

Flowing from the Incarnation, St. Francis had a lively faith in the continuing presence of Jesus in the Church through the sacraments, especially the Eucharist. Before this mystery Francis had a profound awe at the condescension of God, as he also did in God's revealing himself and his truth in Sacred Scripture. Francis had a deep reverence even for the material things connected with Scripture and the sacraments: church buildings, vessels and linens used in Mass, and any paper bearing the name of God or Jesus, as well as the

Bible (the "book") itself. This was not superstition but more a heightened sense of the sacred: a vivid awareness of God incarnated and manifest in these things. All of them loudly proclaimed to him: "God is here!" Thus for Francis, priests in their ministry of preaching and administering the sacraments made the presence of God in Jesus Christ absolutely *luminous* — radiating God's presence and his love.

This is evident in the words Francis wrote or had written in various rules or admonitions:

> We ought indeed to confess all our sins to a priest and receive from him the Body and Blood of our Lord Jesus Christ. He who does not eat his flesh and does not drink his blood cannot enter into the Kingdom of God. Let him, however, eat and drink worthily, because he who receives unworthily "eats and drinks judgment to himself, not discerning the Body of the Lord...."
>
> Let us, moreover, "bring forth fruits worthy of penance."[186]

> Humbly beseech the clergy to venerate above all the most holy Body and Blood of our Lord Jesus Christ and his holy name and written words which sanctify [his] body. They ought to hold as precious the chalices, corporals, ornaments of the altar, and all that pertain to the sacrifice. And if the most holy Body of the Lord be lodged very poorly in any place, let It according to the command of the Church be placed by them and left in a precious place, and let It be carried with great veneration and administered to others with discretion.
>
> The names also and written words of the Lord, whenever they are found in unclean places, let them be collected, and they ought to be put in a proper place. And in all the preaching you do,

admonish the people concerning penance and that no one can be saved except he that receives the most sacred Body and Blood of the Lord. And while It is being sacrificed by the priest on the altar and It is being carried to any place, let all the people on bended knees render praise, honor, and glory to the Lord God living and true.

And you shall so announce and preach his praise to all peoples that at every hour and when the bells are rung, praise and thanks shall always be given to the Almighty God by all the people through the whole earth.[187]

As well as recognizing the sacredness of the Eucharist and the Word of God in Sacred Scripture, St. Francis saw and valued the incarnational dimension in confessing one's sins to a priest and receiving absolution. This has also been underscored frequently by Pope Francis. It was a key theme in some of his general audiences in November 2013. On November 13, Pope Francis emphasized that the sacrament of reconciliation is a "second Baptism," renewing the grace of baptism and thus enabling the faithful to live in the joy of Jesus Christ. In his November 20, 2013, catechesis, the pope said:

> Jesus calls us to live out reconciliation in the ecclesial, the community, dimension.... The Church ... accompanies us on the journey of conversion throughout our life.
>
> Perhaps many do not understand the ecclesial dimension of forgiveness, because individualism, subjectivism, always dominates.... Certainly, God forgives every penitent sinner, personally, but the Christian is tied to Christ, and Christ is united to the Church. For us Christians there is a further gift, there is also a further duty: to pass humbly through the ecclesial community.

We have to appreciate it; it is a gift, a cure, a protection as well.... I go to my brother priest and I say: "Father, I did this...." And he responds: "But I forgive you; God forgives you." At that moment, I am sure that God has forgiven me.... The priest, and he too is a man who, like us in need of mercy, truly becomes the instrument of mercy, bestowing on us the boundless love of God the Father....

Sometimes you hear someone claiming to confess directly to God.... Yes, as I said before, God is always listening, but in the Sacrament of Reconciliation he sends a brother to bestow his pardon, the certainty of forgiveness, in the name of the Church.[188]

So Pope Francis also stresses the incarnational dimension of Catholic life found in the Church's sacraments.

Returning to the incarnational vision of St. Francis, in a "Letter to the Entire Order" written toward the end of his life, Francis testified:

Brother Francis, a worthless and weak man, your very little servant sends his greetings in Him Who has redeemed and *washed us in His* most precious blood. When you hear His name, the name of that *Son of the Most High*, our Lord Jesus Christ, *Who is blessed forever,* adore His name with fear and reverence, *prostrate on the ground! Give praise* to Him *because He is good; exalt Him by your deeds*; for this reason He has sent you into the whole world: that you may bear witness to His voice in word and deed and bring everyone to know that there is *no one who is all-powerful* except Him.

Persevere *in discipline* and holy obedience and, with a good and firm purpose, fulfill what you have promised Him. The Lord *God* offers *Himself* to us as to His *children*.

Kissing your feet, therefore, and with all that love of which I am capable, I implore all of you brothers to show all possible reverence and honor to the most holy Body and Blood of our Lord Jesus Christ in whom that which is in heaven and on earth has been brought to peace and reconciled to almighty God.[189]

When we read the words of St. Francis about Jesus, the Eucharist, the sacraments, Mary and the saints, or any other subject that pertains to the Church or the Catholic faith, one thing is particularly striking: Francis of Assisi did not know or believe anything different than any Catholic of his day ordinarily would know or believe; he just knew and believed it more deeply and passionately. He understood that God deserved the highest praise and reverence, and the things of God deserved the highest honor and respect. He also fervently believed that human salvation hung upon giving God due honor and obeying everything written in Sacred Scripture about salvation.

Francis was not a theologian; he simply encountered God in the great mysteries of faith and in the sacraments with a depth of understanding far beyond that of most Catholics, and in some of the very beliefs (like the presence of Christ in the Eucharist and the sanctity of the priestly office) that many popular heretical and schismatic groups of his time had rejected.

Redemption: *The Suffering and Death of Jesus*

The other Christian belief that was at the heart of St. Francis's grasp of Christianity was his fervent love of the suffering and crucified Redeemer, which led Francis to seek to imitate Jesus in his passion, following him to the cross. This testifies to the fullness and the balance of Francis's Christian life. It is easy to picture Francis as the lover of nature and creation, the buoyant troubadour of the Lord who radiated the joy of Christ, or the devout, sacramental believer who revered Christ's presence in his word and sacrament, while overlooking Francis as one whose greatest desire was to follow and imitate Christ in his suffering. That desire is reflected in the account of perfect joy, where Francis explains to Brother Leo that perfect joy is to experience rejection, beating, and persecution by one's own closest companions and to bear it joyfully for the love of Christ. (We recall that Jesus was betrayed by Judas, turned over for execution by his own people, and denied and forsaken by most of his apostles as he went to the cross.)

Francis sought to embrace poverty because Christ became poor for our sakes, but ironically, poverty itself was not Francis's greatest cross. That, rather, was the misunderstanding and pain he endured from others in his quest to live radical poverty. As one Franciscan scholar observed:

> That ideal vision of the man of poverty and joy who loved nature is one aspect of St. Francis' holiness. But there is another dimension of the holiness of Francis, one which revolves far more around the real facts of life: the trials, the struggles and the suffering he endured in trying to live out his ideal. For Francis sought to live his religious vision in the midst of a society that did not understand or appreciate what he was trying to accomplish.
>
> Even the official leaders of his church struggled to grasp how his vision could possibly be called Christian. They could not understand him; they misunderstood him; they frequently caused him great pain. Francis lived with pain and suffering in his life, he endured it, offered it up, made it a means of his growing identification with the Mystery of Christ.[190]

In spite of its hardship, St. Francis encouraged his disciples to follow Jesus in his suffering. His "Office of the Passion" is an expression of this in the communal prayer of his brothers.[191] In one writing St. Francis echoes St. Paul:

> In what then can you boast? [Then he lists knowledge, wisdom, miracles, and even good looks and riches.] ... [N]othing belongs to you; you can boast in none of these things.
>
> But we can boast in our weaknesses [2 Corinthians 12:5] and in carrying each day the holy cross of our Lord Jesus Christ. Let all of us, brothers, consider the Good Shepherd Who bore the suffering of the cross to save His sheep.
>
> The Lord's sheep followed Him in tribulation and persecution, in shame and hunger, in weakness and temptation, and in other ways; and for these things they received eternal life from the Lord.
>
> Therefore, it is a great shame for us, the servants of God, that the saints have accomplished great things and we want only to receive glory and honor by recounting them.[192]

And later he added:

> Let the brothers remember that they have given themselves and left their bodies for God's sake to the Lord Jesus Christ. For his love they must endure tribulation, persecution and death, because the Lord says: "Whoever loses his life for my sake will save it." "I say to you, my friend, do not be afraid of those who kill the body." "If they persecute you in one city, flee to another."[193]

St. Francis was not afraid of those who could kill the body; in fact, when he went to proclaim the Gospel to the sultan, he was fully prepared to give his life for Christ. In one of his writings, Francis recalled that Jesus' only concern was to do the will of his heavenly Father.

Then he prayed to his Father, saying:

> *Father, if it is possible, let this cup pass away from me* (Matthew 26:39); and his sweat fell to the ground like thick drops of blood (see Luke 22:44). Yet he bowed to his Father's will and said, *Father, thy will be done; yet not as I will, but as thou willest* (Matthew 26:42 and 39). And it was the Father's will that his blessed and glorious Son, whom he gave to us and who was born for our sake, should offer himself by his own blood as a sacrifice and victim on the altar of the cross; and this, not for himself, through whom *all things were made* (John. 1:3), but for our sins, *leaving us an example that we may follow in his steps* (1 Peter 2:21).[194]

Francis followed Jesus faithfully, and the cross seemed to grow heavier as his order continued to diverge from his ideal of poverty and his health failed. Francis sought the face and the will of the Father in all this and journeyed with Brother Leo to pray at the isolated fastness of Mount LaVerna, receiving there the marks of Jesus' crucifixion. The joyful saint had become like his Lord, "a man of sorrows, and acquainted with grief" (Isaiah 53:3). After that, Francis could truly say, like St. Paul, "Henceforth let no man trouble me; for I bear on my body the marks of Jesus" (Galatians 6:17).

A few years ago, while on a study tour in Italy centered on St. Francis, I heard an expert in thirteenth- and fourteenth-century Franciscan art point out that as a result of St. Francis's emphasis on the sufferings of Christ, crucifixes began to portray more graphically Jesus' suffering on the cross: his contorted body, his face etched with pain, and blood flowing copiously (often dripping on the small figures painted at the foot of the cross, such as St. Francis or the patron for whom it was crafted). This was a clear departure from the stylized Byzantine crosses of the time, such as the San Damiano cross in which Jesus is erect, with open eyes and little blood.

Like Jesus, Francis of Assisi came to the end of his life bearing a cross of suffering but with great peace of soul, knowing that he had "finished the race" and "kept the faith" (2 Timothy 4:7). As Jesus gathered his followers in the Upper Room on Holy Thursday and instructed them for the last time before his death, so Francis returned to the Portiuncula, where he was surrounded by his followers as he passed from this life. He was laid naked on the ground, possessing nothing, as he had come into the world.

ST. FRANCIS: ANOINTED BY THE HOLY SPIRIT

The remarkable thing about St. Francis, as we have seen in this chapter, is that in spite of having little or no theological training, this un-theologian expressed in his life and teaching the most profound grasp and seamlessly lived integration of the central mysteries of the Christian faith. He saw the beauty of God reflected in creation and glorified the Lord for it. He was awed by the condescension and love of God in the Incarnation and saw how this coming of God initiated the whole sacramental economy: God's presence in the Catholic Church — in the Eucharist, in the priesthood, in the particular sacraments, and in all the church buildings and sacred vessels that are connected with worship of God.

The incarnation of the Word of God also revealed the fullness of God's message to humanity through Jesus: the fulfillment of all the promises and teaching given by God in the Old Covenant. Francis also understood the meaning and necessity of the suffering and death of Christ for the salvation of the world. He, like St. Paul, gloried in Christ's crucifixion. The final mystery that Francis beautifully expressed in his life and teaching was the victory of Jesus over sin in his resurrection and the sending of the Holy Spirit.

St. Francis's life testified to the vibrant life and power of the risen Lord Jesus and the gift of the Holy Spirit, who is the ultimate source of power for the renewal of the Church that Francis sparked. It was St. Bonaventure, in his *Legenda Maior*, the "authorized" life of St. Francis, who highlighted the power of the Spirit working through Francis in many ways. For example, Bonaventure wrote that after Francis went to live with the lepers after his conversion, he tended them devotedly, kissing their wounds even as he cleaned them of pus and bandaged them, and washed their feet. The Lord blessed him, as a result, with astonishing success in healing the spiritually and physically ill.[195]

Bonaventure proceeded to relate an example of St. Francis healing a person, and later he devoted an entire chapter of his biography to "The Efficacy of His Preaching and His Grace of Healing."[196] In chapter 4 Bonaventure recounts that after Francis had spent a night in prayer:

> When the holy man returned to the friars, he began to probe the secrets of their consciences, to draw courage for them from this wonderful vision and to make many predictions about the growth of the Order. When he disclosed many things that transcended human understanding, the friars realized the *Spirit of the Lord had come to rest* (Isaiah 11:2) upon him in such fullness that it was absolutely safe for them to follow his life and teaching.[197]

Bonaventure later devoted a chapter of his life of Francis (chapter 14) to "His Understanding of Scripture and His Spirit of Prophecy," in which he stated, "[T]he power of the

prophetic spirit in the man of God was certainly extraordi
nary."[198] Bonaventure eloquently summarized this theme:

> The Spirit of the Lord
> who had *anointed and sent* him
> and also *Christ,*
> *the power and the wisdom of God,*
> were with their servant Francis
> *wherever he went*
> so that he might abound
> with words of sound teaching
> and shine
> with miracles of great power.
> For his word
> was like a burning fire
> penetrating the innermost depths of the heart;
> and it filled the minds of all
> with admiration,
> since it made no pretense
> at the elegance of human composition
> but exuded the perfume
> of divine revelation.[199]

Immediately after this, Bonaventure reported that once
when Francis was invited to speak before the pope and the
cardinals, he went blank and could think of nothing to say.
After praying to the Holy Spirit, he began to speak with such
eloquence that it was obvious he spoke not by his own power
but by the Spirit of the Lord (see Acts 6:10).[200]

It may appear that St. Bonaventure's account exhibits
some of the exaggeration of popular hagiography. Even if
this is so, can anyone doubt that St. Francis was anointed in a
particularly powerful manner for the renewal of the Church,
even though he was an ordinary Catholic in many respects?
Francis's primary response to the Holy Spirit was to seek to
live fully the teaching of the Catholic Church and the Word

of God in Sacred Scripture, which is the heart and primary source of the Church's teaching. This resulted in Francis's being used and anointed powerfully by God for the renewal of the Church. Pope Emeritus Benedict XVI reflected on this phenomenon in a meditation on St. Francis he wrote in the early 1990s:

> During the lifetime of Saint Francis of Assisi, people experienced a deep yearning for a Church of the Spirit; they longed for a better, purer, more meaningful Christianity and anticipated that this new Church would bring about a change in the course of history as well. To many of those who suffered from the inadequacies of institutional Christianity, St. Francis seemed to be a God-sent answer to their expectations, and, in fact, Christianity of the Spirit has seldom been so genuinely exemplified as it was in him.
>
> But there was something unusual about him, too. His Christianity of the Spirit was based on an entirely literal obedience to the word of the Bible. The new principle that he opposed to the lukewarm Christianity of casuistry was *sine glossa* (without gloss): he heard the word of God without the barrier of explanations that might serve to moderate it, to make it safe and harmless. He heard it without the academic sophistries that made it an object of controversy for scholars but far removed from the realities of everyday life. He heard it and accepted it as it was, as a word of the Lord addressed to me personally without an "if" or a "but."
>
> And this is the wonderful part: it is the word taken literally that is also the wholly spiritual word. The Spirit appears to be, not in contradiction to the word, but in the word, and the

more deeply we penetrate the word, the more true this becomes.[201]

ST. FRANCIS: LIVING THE WORD OF GOD

Pope Emeritus Benedict XVI (then Cardinal Joseph Ratzinger) put his finger precisely on the secret of St. Francis's renewal of the Catholic Church *and* the key to his life of discipleship: putting into practice (that is, living) the Word of God in its simplest, literal meaning in the power of the Holy Spirit. (It should be noted also that Francis, being a man of humble obedience, lived the Word of God in the power of the Spirit *as the Catholic Church understood it*, not in some novel or esoteric way.) As Pope Francis frequently remarks, St. Francis preached the Gospel with his life, not just with his words. As St. Francis himself wrote in his earliest rule: "Let all the brothers preach with their deeds."[202]

Here is where Francis the saint and Francis the pope are one in their life and in their message. Conversion to Christ and following Christ require *ongoing* conversion that is rooted deeply in prayer — the interior life — but must be manifested in deeds. And the deeds they both stress are those that reach out and touch others, especially the poor and those in need. This would include the materially poor but also those spiritually poor who have not yet discovered God as their loving Father and Jesus as their Savior. Both St. Francis and Pope Francis see and embody with their lives the mission of the Christian to respond to human need in charity *and* to evangelize, that is, to witness to Christ in word and deed.

In addition, both Pope Francis and St. Francis see *repentance* — turning away from sin and turning to God for forgiveness and mercy — as central to the Gospel and urgently needed, both in the thirteenth century and now. Both speak of specific ways that people, and Christians first, need to change their lives (*metanoia*) to conform more fully to the

Gospel. Even though St. Francis preached with his life first, he also was constantly exhorting, teaching, and guiding his followers in how to live the Gospel practically. Even though his dream was to have just the Gospel as his rule, the wisdom of the Church prevailed by helping Francis to specify his Gospel way of life in the rules he composed for his brothers, which contain many specific directions and admonitions based on the Gospel. The Franciscan Rule is an important part of St. Francis's spiritual heritage, which is appropriate for a saint who was so concerned with how one *lives* the Gospel. That's what a *rule* is all about!

POPE FRANCIS: IN THE FOOTSTEPS OF ST. FRANCIS

Pope Francis and St. Francis are both men of great evangelical zeal, burning with fervor for the Gospel and with deep, personal love of the Lord. We know that there are differences too. Pope Francis is a Jesuit, and a Jesuit, almost by definition, is well formed theologically and spiritually through years of study. It would be a misnomer to call Pope Francis an un-theologian. By his very office, the pope is the Church's chief and most authoritative teacher. However, Pope Francis's motto, *Miserando atque Eligendo*, "Lowly but Chosen," indicates that he does not see himself as a great intellectual theologian or philosopher like the two previous popes. But he does know that he has been chosen by God to bring people back home to the Church.[203]

In some ways, Pope Francis's way of communicating the Gospel is very similar to that of his namesake. His preaching style is informal and often conversational. Like St. Francis, he is spontaneous and personally involved with people, often stopping his popemobile to interact with a smile, a word, or an embrace. And although he is well formed theologically, his comments, even to the press, are not always theologically nuanced.[204] His intention is often to call attention to what is pastorally most important and to open the doors to those who may have stopped listening to the Church because they think they know what will be said.

Anyone who has followed Pope Francis's teaching knows that his insights are challenging and unpredictable. Like St. Francis, Pope Francis brings a freshness to the message of Christ. St. Francis showed by his teaching and his life that the Catholic Church could be radically poor and authentic — authentically Christian in an era in which the Catholic Church had grown wealthy and politically powerful. There is this same sort of challenging authenticity in the life and teaching of Pope Francis, as he also is reexamining many of the traditional practices and policies of the papacy and the Catholic Church.

Pope Francis is practical and specific in naming the things that we need to avoid in order to enter the kingdom of heaven, such as worldliness and consumerism, gossip, slander, and hypocrisy. He is especially pointed in his criticism when Church law and custom are administered in ways that lack compassion and end up alienating people from Christ and his Church. In his own way, like St. Francis in his time, Pope Francis is calling people to repentance. His emphasis, though, is on the mercy of God — the fact that God always goes ahead of us to extend mercy. The pope illustrates this most poignantly in his exposition of the parable of the merciful father, that is, the parable of the prodigal son.

Like St. Francis, Pope Francis reaches out to people on the outskirts, as we have seen. He, like St. Francis, desires a poor Church for the poor, and he challenges us by his lifestyle as well as by his teaching to look at our own lives and consider how we could imitate more closely the "poor Christ" — an ideal that was so central to Francis of Assisi.

Though challenging, the message of Pope Francis does not lead the person open to hearing the truth into depression, condemnation, or discouragement, because he points to the merciful love of God the Father, who is always ready to forgive. Also, Pope Francis, like St. Francis, *encourages* simply because of the joy and hope of the messenger. This, for St. Francis, was exquisitely presented in a reflection on the impact of the saint in the first biography of Thomas of Celano — a reflection that immediately precedes a very thorough physical description of Francis. This literary portrait of Francis's virtues captures, far better than the precise physical description, the impact and spirit of the saint and the impression he left on his followers:

> How handsome,
> how splendid!
> How *gloriously he appeared*
> in innocence of life,
> in simplicity of words,
> in purity of heart,
> in love of God,
> in fraternal charity,
> in enthusiastic obedience,
> in agreeable compliance,
> *in angelic appearance.*
> Friendly in behavior,
> serene in nature,
> affable in speech,
> generous in encouragement,
> *faithful in commitment,*
> prudent in advice,
> efficient in endeavor,
> he was *gracious in everything!*
> Tranquil in mind,
> pleasant in disposition,
> *sober in spirit,*
> lifted in contemplation,
> tireless in prayer,

he was fervent in everything!
Firm in intention,
consistent in virtue,
persevering in grace,
he was the same in everything!
Swift to forgive,
slow to grow angry,
free in nature,
remarkable in memory,
subtle in discussing,
careful in choices,
he was simple in everything!
Strict with himself,
kind with others,
he was discerning in everything![205]

Yes, Pope Francis did well in choosing for his papal name such a beloved and illustrious saint, one who has appealed to many people for centuries and who is powerful in showing us the meaning of conversion to Christ and how to follow Jesus in the way of Christian discipleship. Amid the tensions and confusions of issues and ideologies in the modern world, it is good to recall the witness of a saint who radiated and lived the teaching of Jesus in such a passionate and simple way, reminding us that how we live is the truest measure of our faith.

Pope Francis, as his pontificate demonstrates, is directing the Church to examine how we are living the gospel of Christ and whether we are experiencing the saving mercy of God revealed most fully in Jesus. In Christ we have great joy and hope, a joy and hope that we Christians must share with others by our lives.

Pope Francis is also inviting the world that does not yet believe in Jesus Christ to consider the beauty and truth of the Son of God and his saving and liberating message. I can think of no better close to this book than a prayer of St.

Francis, which the oldest collection of Francis's writings (Assisi Codex 338) places at the end of his Letter to the Entire Order:

> Almighty, eternal, just and merciful God,
> grant us in our misery
> that we may do for your sake alone
> what we know you want us to do,
> and always want what pleases you;
> so that, cleansed and enlightened interiorly
> and fired with the ardor of the Holy Spirit,
> we may be able to follow
> in the footsteps of your Son,
> our Lord Jesus Christ,
> and so make our way to you,
> Most High,
> by your grace alone,
> you who live and reign
> in perfect Trinity and simple Unity,
> and are glorified,
> God all-powerful,
> for ever and ever.
> Amen.[206]

NOTES

1 Hans Urs von Balthasar, *Razing the Bastions*, trans. Brian McNeil, C.R.V. (San Francisco: Ignatius, 1993), p. 32.

2 Pope Francis, Interview with Andrea Tornielli, December 14, 2013, in *La Stampa*, www.lastampa.it.

3 Ibid.

4 G.K. Chesterton, *St. Francis of Assisi* (Garden City, N.Y.: Doubleday, 1957), pp. 96–97.

5 Pope Francis, Address to Representatives of the Communications Media, March 16, 2013, www.vatican.va.

6 Augustine Thompson, O.P., *Francis of Assisi: A New Biography* (Ithaca, N.Y./London: Cornell University Press, 2012), pp.154, 155. Thompson presents a thorough overview of the state of scholarship on the Franciscan Question in a chapter with this title. pp. 153–170.

7 Andre Vauchez, *Francis of Assisi: The Life and After Life of a Medieval Saint*, trans. Michael F. Cusato (New Haven, Conn./ London: Yale University Press, 2012), p. xi.

8 Ibid., p. xxi.

9 Thompson quotes a recent scholar, Jacque Dalarun, who "has rightly called [the *Fioretti*] the 'combat manual' of fourteenth-century schismatic (and of often heretical) Franciscans." Thompson, *Francis of Assisi*, p. 156.

10 Thompson is convinced that the taming of the wolf of Gubbio is just a tale. See *Francis of Assisi*, p. viii.

11 "The Anonymous of Perugia," 4, "The Legend of the Three Companions," 3, in *Francis of Assisi: Early Documents*, vol.2. "The Founder," 35, 69. Also see "The First Life of St. Francis" by Thomas Celano, 17, in *Early Documents*, vol. 1, "The Saint," pp. 195, 196. Chesterton dramatizes this incident in *Francis of Assisi*, p. 41.

12 "Legend of the Three Companions," 6, in *Early Documents*, vol. 2, p. 71.

13 Chesterton, *Francis of Assisi*, p. 43.

14 Pope Francis, homily, April 14, 2013, www.vatican.va.

15 The "Legend of the Three Companions," no. 3, testifies, "He was naturally courteous in manner and speech and, following his heart's intent, never uttered a rude or offensive word to anyone." *Early Documents*, vol. 2, p. 69.

16 The "Legend of the Three Companions," no. 4, in *Early Documents*, vol. 2, p. 70.

17 Pope Francis, "Q & A with Students," in *Origins*, June 27, 2013, vol. 43, no. 8, p. 114.

18 Ibid., p. 115.

19 Ibid.

20 Vigil of Pentecost with the Ecclesial Movements, May 18, 2013, www.vatican.va.

21 Francesca Ambrogetti and Sergio Rubin, *Pope Francis: His Life in His Own Words* (New York: G.P. Putnam Sons, 2013), p. 34.

22 Pope Francis, Pentecost Vigil, May 18, 2013, www.vatican.va.

23 *Medieval Sourcebook: The Testament of St. Francis*, trans. by David Burr, www.fordham.edu.

24 Thomas of Celano, "First Life of St. Francis," 3, in *Early Documents*, vol. 1, p. 184.

25 Thompson, p. 10.

26 Celano, "First Life of St. Francis," 3, 4 in *Early Documents*, vol. 1, p. 185.

27 Thompson, p. 177.

28 Thompson, p. 11.

29 Thompson, p. 12.

30 Pope Francis, Homily for the Third Sunday of Easter, April 14, 2013, www.vatican.va.

31 Pope Francis, homily, June 14, 2013, www.vatican.va.

32 Thompson, p. 13.

33 www.franciscanfriarstor.com, *Franciscan Prayer Book*. This prayer is reminiscent of Newman's famous prayer in a time of spiritual struggle and searching, "Lead, Kindly Light."

34 Thompson, pp. 13, 14.

35 *Medieval Sourcebook: The Testament of St. Francis*, trans. by David Burr, www.fordham.edu.

36   Thompson, p. 17.

37   Thompson, p. 16: "This encounter with lepers, not the act of stripping off his clothing before the bishop, would always be for Francis the core of his religious conversion."

38   Manselli, p. 63.

39   Manselli, pp. 85, 86.

40   The sign of the true Christian as the one who "steps outside" of himself or herself and reaches out in real practical ways to the poor or marginalized is stated in many of Pope Francis's first homilies and audiences given, for example, in 2013 on March 27 (1st general audience), April 24, May 8, May 18, July 8 (at Lampedusa), and more.

41   Pope Francis, "Q and A with Students", *Origins*, June 27, 2013, p. 114.

42   Ibid.

43   St. Bonaventure, "Life of St. Francis," in *Bonaventure* (New York: Paulist, 1978), p. 188.

44   *Pope Francis: Conversation with Jorge Bergoglio*, Sergio Rubin and Francesca Ambrogetti, ed. (New York: Putnam, 2010), p. 42.

45   St. Bonaventure recounts that this event took place one day when Francis was out walking and meditating. He came upon the church of San Damiano, and feeling inspired by the Holy Spirit, he went in to pray. *Bonaventure*, p. 191.

46   *Pope Francis: Conversation with Jorge Bergoglio*, p. 45.

47   *Bonaventure*, "Life of St. Francis," p. 202.

48   Ibid., p. 216.

49   Francis explains his rationale for desiring to devote himself to prayer over preaching, and it is very similar to Jesus' praise of Mary's (of Bethany) vocation over Martha's. Also Francis says that "I am a simple man, and unskilled in speech." See *Bonaventure*, pp. 291, 292, 294.

50   Ibid., p. 273.

51   Quoted in Raniero Cantalamessa, *Come, Creator Spirit* (Collegeville, Minn., Liturgical, 2003), p. 226, citing Celano,

First Life, 7.16 (Early Documents, I, p. 194), *Second Life*, 8.13 (*Early Documents*, II, p. 252).

52 *Bonaventure*, "Life of St. Francis," pp. 274–275.

53 *Bonaventure*, "Life of St. Francis," pp. 273–278.

54 Ibid., pp. 208, 209.

55 Vatican II, *Sacrosanctum Concilium*, art. 12.

56 Jorge Bergoglio, *Pope Francis: His Life in His Own Words*, pp. 45, 46.

57 John Paul II, *Crossing the Threshold of Hope* (New York: Alfred A. Knopf, 1994), p. 16.

58 Francis of Assisi, *Early Documents*, vol. 1, p. 158.

59 Ibid., pp. 158–159.

60 Fr. Pascal Robinson, O.F.M., *The Writings of St. Francis of Assisi* (Philadelphia: Dolphin, 2006). Language updated to reflect contemporary usage.

61 Ibid.

62 Ibid.

63 Francis of Assisi, *Early Documents*, vol. 1, p. 163.

64 Robinson.

65 Francis of Assisi, *Early Documents*, vol. 1, p. 141.

66 www.franciscanfriarstor.com, adapted from *Franciscan Prayer Book*.

67 Robinson.

68 Francis of Assisi, *Early Documents*, vol. 1, pp. 116–118.

69 Marion A. Habig, ed., *St. Francis of Assisi Omnibus of Sources*, (Quincy, Ill.: Franciscan Press, 1991), p. 67.

70 Francis of Assisi, *Early Documents*, vol. 1, pp. 116–118.

71 Sean Cardinal O'Malley, Foreword to *In Him Alone is Our Hope*, Jorge Mario Bergoglio's Spiritual Exercises given to his brother bishops (New York: Magnificat, 2013), p. 7.

72 Pope Francis, @Pontifex, twitter.com/Pontifex, March 17, 2013.

73 Howard Chua-Eon and Elizabeth Dias, "The People's Pope," *Time* magazine, December 23, 2013, p. 72.

74 Ibid.

75 Mario Ponzi, "An act of love for Noemi," *L'Osservatore Romano*, Eng. ed., November 8, 2013, p. 1.

76 Pope Francis, "Peaceful Resolution needed in Syria," *Origins*, vol. 43, no. 15 (September 12, 2013), p. 230.

77 Pope Francis. Homily at Mass, Monday, September 9, 2013, www.vatican.va.

78 Taken from Jorge Bergoglio and Abraham Skorka, *On Heaven and Earth* (2011), quoted in Mario Escobar, *Francis: Man of Prayer* (Nashville: Thomas Nelson, 2013), p. 171.

79 Pope Francis, homily, December 6, 2013, www.vatican.va.

80 Pope Francis, General Audience, May 15, 2013, www.vatican.va.

81 As noted by Cardinal Sean O'Malley, Foreword to *In Him Alone is Our Hope*, Jorge Mario Bergoglio's Spiritual Exercises given to his brother bishops (New York: Magnificat, 2013), p. 7.

82 Reflections on Pope Francis by Michael Kelly, S.J., reported in *Pray for Me: The Life and Spiritual Vision of Pope Francis, the First Pope from the Americas* (Colorado Springs, CO. Image, 2013), pp. 167, 168.

83 See, for example, "The Anonymous of Perugia," chap. 3, no 14: "… [H]aving no place to stay, they went and found a poor and nearly abandoned church called St. Mary of the Portiuncula. There they built a small dwelling where they all lived together." (*Early Documents*, vol. 2, p. 39)

84 See "Legend of the Three Companions," chap. 8, no. 29, in *Early Documents*, vol. 22, p. 86, and "The Anonymous of Perugia," chap. 2, no. 11, in *Early Documents*, vol. 2, p. 38.

85 "The Earlier Rule," in *Early Documents*, vol. 1, pp. 63, 64.

86 "A Salutation of the Virtues," in *Early Documents*, vol. 1, p. 164.

87 Thomas of Celano, (First) "Life of St. Francis," chap. 9, sec. 22, in *Early Documents*, vol. 1, pp. 201, 202.

88 "The Anonymous of Perugia," 28, 29, in *Early Documents*, vol. 2, p. 47.

89 "The Testament," lines 14–22, in *Early Documents*, vol. 1, pp. 125, 126

90   "The Earlier Rule," chap. 9, lines 1–5, in *Early Documents*, vol. 1, p. 70.

91   "Before this faith can be exercised, man must have the grace of God to move and assist him; he must have the interior help of the Holy Spirit, who moves the heart and converts it to God, who opens the eyes of the mind and 'makes it easy for all to accept and believe the truth.'" Vatican II, *Dei Verbum*, no. 5, in Austin Flannery, OP, ed., *Vatican Council II: The Conciliar and Post Conciliar Documents* (Northport, N.Y.: Costello, 1975), p. 752.

92   Pope Francis, "Q and A with Students," in *Origins*, June 27, 2013, p. 117.

93   Pope Francis, "Pentecost Vigil: Jesus, Prayer, Witness," May 18, 2013, www.vatican.va.

94   Ibid.

95   Ibid.

96   Ibid.

97   "Revolutionaries of Grace" in *L'Osservatore Romano*, English ed., June 26, 2013, no. 26, p. 12.

98   Pope Francis, "Money must serve, not rule," in *L'Osservatore Romano*, English ed., May 22, 2013 (no. 21), pp. 5–6.

99   Quoted in "Lady Poverty and Lady Economy," in *L'Osservatore Romano*, English ed., August 6, 2013, pp. 6, 13.

100   *Medieval Sourcebook: The Testament of St. Francis*, trans. David Burr, www.fordham.edu.

101   Thompson, pp. 30, 31.

102   Thompson, p. 33.

103   Francis of Assisi, *Early Documents*, vol. 1, p. 42.

104   Francis of Assisi, *Early Documents*, vol. 1, p. 63.

105   Ibid. See pp. 64–71, 75–76, 80–81.

106   Pope Francis, General Audience, May 29, 2013, www.vatican.va.

107   www.patheos.com.

108   Pope Francis, homily, May 18, 2013. Also, in a Wednesday audience on June 19, 2013, Pope Francis said, "Unity is a grace for which we must ask the Lord that he may liberate us from

the temptation of division, of conflict between us, of selfishness, of gossip. How much evil gossip does, how much evil! Never gossip about others, never!" www.vatican.va.

109 Pope Francis, homily, Pentecost, May 29, 2013, www.vatican.va.

110 Pope Francis, General Audience, June 19, 2013, www.vatican.va.

111 Pope Francis, General Audience, May 29, 2013, www.vatican.va.

112 Pope Francis, Address to Families of the World on Pilgrimage for the Year of Faith, October 28, 2013. www.zenit.org.

113 Pope Francis, "Christian acceptance," *L'Osservatore Romano*, English ed., May 29, 2013 (no. 22), p. 13.

114 Pope Francis, homily, Inaugural Mass, March 19, 2013, www .vatican.va.

115 Pope Francis, Visit to Lampedusa, homily, July 8, 2013, www .vatican.va.

116 Pope Francis, Visit to Lampedusa, July 8, 2013, www.vatican.va.

117 Omer Englebert, *St. Francis of Assisi: A Biography* (Ann Arbor, Mich.: Servant, 1979), pp. 58, 59.

118 Ibid., p. 61.

119 Francis of Assisi, *Early Documents*, vol. 1, p. 77.

120 *Early Documents*, vol. 1, p. 47.

121 Habig, pp. 67–68.

122 Robinson.

123 Pope Francis, "A Big Heart Open to God," Antonio Spadaro, S.J., *America* magazine, September 30, 2013.

124 Robinson.

125 "The Assisi Compilation," chap. 18 in *Francis of Assisi, Early Documents*, vol.2, pp. 132–133.

126 Thomas of Celano, "Second Life of St. Francis," chap. 108 in *Francis of Assisi, Early Documents,* vol.2, p. 342.

127 Pope Francis, General Audience, May 29, 2013, www.vatican.va.

128 Pope Francis, "Meeting with the Clergy, Consecrated People and Members of Diocesan Pastoral Councils," Cathedral of San Rufino, Assisi, Italy, October 4, 2013, www.vatican.va.

129 Pope Francis, "A Big Heart Open to God," Antonio Spadaro, S.J., *America* magazine, September 30, 2013.

130   Pope Francis, General Audience, October 2, 2013, www.vatican.va.

131   Pope Francis, homily, September 17, 2013, www.vatican.va.

132   Jorge Mario Bergoglio (Pope Francis), *In Him Alone Is Our Hope* (New York: Magnificat, 2013), p. 29.

133   Pope Francis, homily, October 7, 2013, www.vatican.va.

134   Owen Chadwick, *The Reformation* (Baltimore, Md.: Penguin, 1964), p. 257.

135   Pope Francis, interview, "A Big Heart Open to God," Antonio Spadaro, S.J., *America* magazine, September 30, 2013.

136   Ibid.

137   Pope Francis, "Homily of Holy Father Francis" during his Pastoral Visit to Assisi, October 4, 2013, www.vatican.va.

138   Message of Pope Francis for World Mission Day 2013, www .vatican.va.

139   Thompson, p. 27.

140   Thompson, pp. 42.

141   Ibid., *Francis of Assisi: Early Documents*, vol. 1, p. 78.

142   *Francis of Assisi: Early Documents*, vol. 1, p. 78.

143   Ibid., p. 57.

144   *Lumen Gentium*, no. 25. See also *Christus Dominus*, no. 12.

145   Pope Francis, homily, October 25, 2013, www.vatican.va.

146   See the Decree on the Church's Missionary Activity (*Ad gentes divinitus*), no. 2, one of the most frequently overlooked documents of the Second Vatican Council.

147   Thompson, pp. 66–69.

148   Pope Francis, Homily on Feast of St. Francis of Assisi, October 4, 2013, www.vatican.va.

149   Pope Francis, General Audience, March 27, 2013, www.vatican .va.

150   Pope Francis, "A Big Heart Open to God," Antonio Spadaro, S.J., *America* magazine, September 30, 2013.

151   Pope Francis, Address to Clergy, Consecrated People and Members of Diocesan Pastoral Councils, Cathedral of San Rutino, Assisi, October 4, 2013, www.vatican.va.

152 Pope Francis, "Listening to the Wounds of Jesus," *L'Osservatore Romano*, English ed., October 9, 2013, no. 41, pp. 7, 8.

153 Pope Francis, "For a Church Stripped of Worldliness," October 4, 2013, *L'Osservatore Romano*, English ed., no. 41, p.9.

154 Pope Francis, "Proclaim the Gospel and if necessary use words," October 4, 2013. *L'Osservatore Romano*, English ed., no. 41, pp. 13, 14.

155 Ibid.

156 Pope Francis, General Audience, May 22, 2013, www.vatican.va.

157 Ibid.

158 Pope Francis, Angelus Address, December 15, 2013. www.vatican .va.

159 Chesterton, *Francis of Assisi*, p. 81.

160 *Mirror of Perfection*, 96. Downloaded from portiunculathelittle portion.blogspot.com.

161 Pope Francis, Angelus, December 16, 2013, www.zenit.org.

162 Francis of Assisi, *Earlier Rule*, chapter 7, in *Francis of Assisi, Early Documents*, vol. 1, p. 69.

163 *Francis of Assisi, Early Documents*, vol. 1, p. 194.

164 *The Little Flowers of St. Francis* (New York: Doubleday Image, 1958), pp. 60–62, 319, 320.

165 G.K. Chesterton, *Francis of Assisi*, p. 77.

166 Omer Englebert, *Francis of Assisi*, pp. 227, 228.

167 St. Augustine, *Confessions*, trans. Henry Chadwick (Oxford University Press, 1992), p. 3.

168 Pope Francis, *Only Love Can Save Us: Letters, Homilies, and Talks of Cardinal Jorge Bergoglio* (Huntington, Ind.: Our Sunday Visitor, 2013), pp. 67, 69.

169 Cardinal Jorge Bergoglio, "Projecting the Joy of Faith," Letter to Catechists of the Archdiocese of Buenos Aires, August 21, 2012, in *Pope Francis: Encountering Christ* (New Rochelle, N.Y.: Scepter, 2013), pp. 22, 23.

170 Cardinal Jorge Bergoglio, "Anointed with the Oil of Gladness," Homily at the Chrism Mass, Buenos Aires, April 21, 2011, in *Encountering Christ*, pp. 104–107.

171   Cardinal Jorge Bergoglio, "Savoring the Joy of Christ," Homily on the Solemnity of Corpus Christi, June 25, 2011, in *Encountering Christ*, pp. 83–85.

172   Pope Francis, Palm Sunday Homily, March 24, 2013, www.vatican .va.

173   Pope Francis, homily, December 3, 2013, www.vatican.va.

174   Pope Francis, homily, May 31, 2013, www.vatican.va.

175   Ibid.

176   Pope Francis, homily, May 10, 2013. www.vatican.va.

177   Ibid.

178   Pope Francis, homily, September 6, 2013, www.vatican.va.

179   Pope Francis, "Authentic and Consistent," *L'Osservatore Romano*, English ed., July 17, 2013, no 29, pp. 6–7.

180   Pope Francis, Address to Seminarians and Novices, posted July 10, 2013, www.zenit.net.

181   Pope Francis, general audience, June 26, 2013, www.vatican.va.

182   *Evangelii Gaudium*, no. 3. All quotes from Evangelii Gaudium are from the Vatican web site: www.vatican.va. Quote is from Paul VI, Apostolic Exhortation *Gaudete in Domino* (May 9, 1975), no. 22.

183   Pope Francis, General Audience, May 22, 2013, www.vatican.va.

184   Francis wrote on begging for alms in his Early Rule: "Alms are a legacy and a justice due to the poor that our Lord Jesus Christ acquired for us. The brothers who work at acquiring them will receive a great reward and enable those who give them to gain and acquire one; for all that people leave behind in the world will perish, but they will have a reward from the Lord for the charity and almsgiving they have done. *Francis of Assisi, Early Documents*, vol. 1, pp. 70–71.

185   Matthias Neumann, O.S.B., "The Holiness of St. Francis: Spiritual Vision and Lived Suffering." *Review for Religious*, September/October 1985, p. 684.

186   Robinson.

187   Ibid.

188 Pope Francis, General Audience, November 20, www.vatican .va.

189 *Francis of Assisi, Early Documents,* vol. 1, pp. 116, 117.

190 Matthias Neumann, O.S.B, "The Holiness of St. Francis," p. 681.

191 *Francis of Assisi, Early Documents,* vol. 1, pp. 137–148.

192 Ibid., p. 131.

193 Ibid., p. 95.

194 Habig, p. 93.

195 *Bonaventure,* "Life of St. Francis," p. 195.

196 Ibid., pp. 291 ff.

197 Ibid., pp. 209–210.

198 Ibid., p. 284.

199 Ibid., 297.

200 Ibid., 297, 298.

201 Joseph Ratzinger, *Co-Workers of the Truth: Meditations for Every Day of the Year,* trans. M.F. McCarthy and L. Krauth, ed. I. Grassl (San Francisco: Ignatius, 1992), pp. 323, 324.

202 Francis of Assisi, *Early Documents,* vol. 1, pp. 95, 75.

203 Fr. Gabriel Gillen, O.P., in *The Trumpet* (a quarterly newsletter of the Dominican Foundation, Dominican friars, Province of St. Joseph), Fall, 2013, 2.

204 Such as his in-flight press interview after World Youth Day in Brazil in August 2013.

205 Thomas of Celano, "The (First) Life of St. Francis," First Book, Chapter XXIX, *ED,* Vol. 1, 252–253.

206 Habig, p. 108.